Immigration
in Modern Times

the What, the Where & the How
A Personal Story and Critique

PATRICK CHU

Editing, design, typesetting and publishing by UK Book Publishing

www.ukbookpublishing.com

ISBN: 978-1-915338-38-9

Cover photo: © killian Pham – Unsplash

CONTENTS

A SPECIAL NOTE

I finished the manuscript of this book around mid-March of 2022, and had planned to submit to my publisher in late March. However, a major global event happened which compelled me to add this special note, which may have some resonance with this book.

On 24 February 2022, Russia sent in what was termed by President Putin as a special military operation into neighbouring Ukraine. Other countries around the world called this an invasion. Ukraine is a country which gained its independence in 1991. Since then, Ukraine is recognized as a sovereign country that has diplomatic recognition by nearly all the 193 member states (except eight) of the United Nations.

That date marked an unprecedented event. Russia, the biggest country (by land area) in the world, invaded the second-biggest country (by land area) in Europe, Ukraine. The two countries share a long border. On that day, Russia invaded its neighbour. Western intelligence had been warning for weeks about the invasion, while Russia had on record denied the plan for an invasion, stating that the military build-up along the border was a military exercise.

According to Putin's view of history, Ukraine, as a sovereign country, should never have existed. He thinks that people from both countries belong to the Slavic race, and therefore, Ukraine should be restored as part of Mother Russia, as was the case before the dissolution of the Soviet Union in 1991.

The world watched in horror at the devastation wrought by the Russian military. Within three weeks, the military conflict has resulted in more than two million refugees from Ukraine moving westward towards other countries, in particular, Poland. It is estimated by the United Nations that there may be up to five million refugees, mostly women, the elderly and children. This would be the biggest refugee crisis the world has ever seen in the 21st century. Ukrainian males of fighting age were barred from leaving Ukraine. They were asked to stay behind and fight to protect their country.

In face of this humanitarian crisis, all the member states of the European Union, together with the UK, which is now outside the EU, expressed unanimous solidarity in receiving and helping these refugees.

In the years to come, history will show that this willingness of all to receive and help the refugees will be the stand-out chapter of humanity and solidarity in this war. It will prove once again that we humans have in the very nature of our being an unshakable desire to help each other in times of need. Victory is not defined by territory gained, but by the human spirits shown, so aptly and movingly demonstrated by Europeans helping other Europeans in need.

PREFACE

I t is every writer's wish that in writing a book, the readers, however many or few, will read the book in its entirety. This is my wish too. Yet, in these days of fast and instant messaging, where social platform is the norm for spreading opinions and views, where messages are judged by their brevity, wittiness, theatrics and, above all, its punchline, then such wish may seem fanciful to an amateur like me.

In 2018, it was reported that only 16% of participants in the Goodreads Reading Challenge actually completed it, finishing only 21% of the total books pledged. The split between fiction and non-fiction of the 16% was not known, though one would guess most readers will be attracted more by fiction than non-fiction.

Many would agree that a common reading habit is to look at the cover and the title, then the introductory and concluding chapters. Certainly, this is no different from my own habit. Being a practising medical doctor, in reading any clinical papers published in the peer reviewed medical journals, I often tend to read the abstract and the conclusion before I decide to read the whole text.

Therefore, I do not anticipate that there would be many readers who are likely to read this book from page to page.

Out of respect for this common reading habit, I have intentionally chosen to give each chapter a fairly distinctive heading. In so doing, some key contents, such as Brexit and the USA immigration policy, may demonstratively appear to be slightly repetitive in nature. This is done to ensure that the reader can skip from chapter to chapter and still be connected with the main flavour of the views expressed in this book.

In addition, I have also put in some of my very personal and cherished experiences, where appropriate, of being an immigrant myself, not only once, but twice.

Migration is an expression of the human aspiration
for dignity, safety and a better future,

It is part of the social fabric, part of our
very make-up as a human family

Ban Ki-moon

Secretary General of the United Nations

2007-2016

CHAPTER 1

Why I write this book

This will be a short book. It is not a book reflecting the work of academics, such as political scientists, economists, sociologists. I am afraid I am none of these and therefore by no means as qualified as they are in writing about immigration. I am, however, an immigrant myself. In my audacious attempt to write this book, it is not my intention either to generate widespread interest and debates, but to seek a plausible explanation of events. The shapers and doers of things in the international arena may not even notice this book, let alone attempt to read it.

This book, however, is my attempt to share my own personal views with those who may have been, or are planning to be, an immigrant at some stage, wherever they may be. In other words, it is a very honest endeavour to share my stories with them and in doing so, provide them with some practical, and hopefully useful, insights.

In writing this book, I am mainly referring to legal immigrants as defined and accepted by the host country to which the emigrants aspire to move. The issues of undocumented migrants, otherwise commonly known in the public press as illegal immigrants, or those seeking political asylum, will not be discussed in this book. The discussion on these latter groups is far too controversial, emotional, and is often seen through the lens of geopolitics, on which I am singularly unqualified to pass a comment. These groups typically have humanitarian implications as well, on which a cool and rational discussion can be very challenging, if not impossible.

This book will also try to provide some views to explain why some countries recently are active in welcoming certain immigrants, especially people from Hong Kong. Would such a welcome lead to an easier and more successful assimilation in the host countries? What should be the right attitude for those who choose to become immigrants? Is there anything in my own experience as an immigrant all those years ago that could be shared?

Immigration is simplistically viewed by many as basically a binary process, those who move and those who receive. Yet, it is not as simple as that. It is far more complex. The binary process would cease to be binary when immigrants from various places all choose the same country as their destination.

Each group of immigrants will manifestly come and bring with them their own culture, religious belief, and lifestyle. Once all these are factored in together, it is no longer binary, and assimilation of the immigrants into the host country will be very complicated and time-consuming. True assimilation, by necessity, is insidious in nature, and will take years to achieve.

For these reasons, I will confine the main focus of the book to be on describing the waves of emigration from Hong Kong. I shall also try to explore and explain the reasons behind these waves from the social and economic points of view. I will stay away from the politics of immigration as much as possible, which I am of course unqualified to write about. I will, however, attempt to address the larger picture of immigration by touching on the general aspects of immigration in the international arena.

I have also tried to speak to as many recent immigrants from Hong Kong as possible. I need to hear their stories, so I can get a feel for why they move and what sort of problems they face. I also have talked to many immigrants from China as well, most of whom are people I previously worked with in the UK. Many of them have settled down and are working in various sectors, including universities, health services, restaurants, Chinese supermarkets and private enterprises.

There are not that many books on immigration available in the mass market of the publishing world. Partly, I think, this is not something that non-immigrants are particularly interested in, unless of course the scale of the immigration is such that it is perceived as having an impact on the social equilibrium of a particular host country.

Yet, immigration is often used as a political tool, most strikingly, as a short-term vote winning tactic during political campaigns. It can be an effective tool, nonetheless. The absolute classical illustrations of this were when the UK held a referendum in 2016 on the issue of its membership of the EU (European Union), a process now known as Brexit, and the USA stance on immigration from Mexico when President Donald Trump was running for the US presidency in the same year. Immigration, or more to the point, the clampdown on immigration, was for both countries very high on the agenda for national debate. Outside these election cycles, most discussions on immigration tend to be from learned institutions such as think tanks or universities.

I also notice that in the two examples I just outlined, the popular press was quick to jump onto the bandwagon on the perils of immigration, to flame an easily inflammable sentiment. They added fuel to the fire, so to speak, simplistically reducing it to a phenomenon that more foreigners arriving must mean that more jobs, resources and opportunities for the local people would be displaced, as if it is a zero-sum game. In reading around this subject of immigration, I also found that published discussions tended to focus on particular host countries, which by and large means those countries in the English-speaking world. This of course is understandable, as each country should have its own way of dealing with immigration. One thing was noticeable: there was hardly anything published in reference to Hong Kong.

If truth be told, the success and the story of Hong Kong is in itself a story of immigration. These days, Hong Kong has always been regarded as a city of international fame and achievements, so many do not see immigration or emigration as a problem for such a city, let alone discussing it. In fact, to control the population growth, the Hong Kong Special Administrative Region (SAR) government does have a tight immigration policy, though it does not have an emigration policy. The city has always been a free international port with freedom to enter and exit.

Another personal reason for writing this book, quite by accident and luck, is a suggestion from a close friend, whom I also regard as a mentor. Out of my respect for him, I shall not mention his name. He is a very experienced and successful writer as well as an editor. So, even though I am not a professional writer, he suggested that I should write a book on this, especially since I can approach this both as an immigrant into the UK, where I now live, and as an emigrant from Hong Kong, where I grew up.

The final reason for writing this book is, by using such a narrowly defined narrative, I can devote it to the people of Hong Kong. Many of them, almost without exception, will have families or friends who were, or are, immigrants themselves, especially from China, or emigrants to other host countries.

So, if the readers have the impression that this book's narrative is too focused on Hong Kong or Greater China on the issue of immigration, they would have no argument from me.

Before I started writing this book, I cross-checked the contact lists of my friends from primary school, secondary school and university. I found that no less than 30% of them are now residing abroad. For those who remain in Hong Kong, many of them hold foreign passports.

It is for these reasons that I write this book, which is dedicated to the people of Hong Kong who have overcome, with great courage and resourcefulness, the challenges of immigration when they or their parents came to Hong Kong all those years ago.

I fully admit that I am no expert in this field. I therefore cannot offer any authoritative discussion on this very important social topic. My views can be wrong, misinterpreted, and certainly disagreed with. Nonetheless, I can reassure the readers that, if for nothing else, I write with sincerity and honesty, which I hope can make up for the shortcomings of this book.

CHAPTER 2

Brexit and Hong Kong
– a unique opportunity

I first started the idea of this book in the summer of 2021. Ever since we entered the new millennium some 21 years ago, the topic and the trends of global immigration has attracted much international attention and debate among the politicians, economists and sociologists, sitting always near the top of the agenda in many election campaigns for leaders of states. The younger electorate, often labelled as Generation X or the Millennials, may come to view this as a trend that matters only to the politicians. Not so, the debates on immigration happened at least 200 years ago, when sea travel supplemented land travel as a means for human movement. The landmark here being the founding of the USA in 1776, when this new Republic exerted its magnetic pull for Europeans onto its East Coast, the Asians onto its West Coast and the Latinos at its Southern border.

So, immigration itself is not something new. It was regarded by most historians as the same social phenomenon which has occurred throughout human civilization, except it was called migration then. The history of nation states throughout history can be very difficult to figure out and may even be confusing, as borders were often ill-defined, subject to wars and invasions. The borders, if they did exist, would depend on who conquered or defeated whom through battles for territorial gain and possession, be it countries or empires. Therefore, one of the chapters in this book will be on the history of human migration, which gradually metamorphosised to immigration. Migration, as a human endeavour, started ever since the dawn of civilization, but it slowly evolves into a process of what we now know as immigration, as it involves the permission to enter and settle down in a chosen country through a process of application and then the granting of an entry visa by the host country.

Since the millennium, immigration trend has taken a new direction. Inevitably, therefore, the debate on immigration has also become more heated in nearly all the countries which are popular host countries. These discussions in general are heavily biased towards the views of the host countries such as the USA, the UK or a bloc of countries such as the European Union (EU). So it can mean those who wish to go to the USA, Australia, Canada or the UK, or those outside the EU applying for entry into an EU member state.

Most of these countries of destinations (also known as host countries) are modern democracies which hold regular general elections so that the electorate can choose which candidates on whom they can cast their votes, based on what the politicians say in their manifesto during their campaign. Without exception, immigration has thus been exploited by some politicians as a means of getting populist support. Immigration, or rather, the restraint on immigration, is seen by political opportunists as an easy way to gain votes. It shifts the blame on any failings of any state, such as unemployment, to the foreigners, who are seen to have taken jobs from the locals, even though most of these are low paid jobs rejected by the locals. Allegedly, the availability of social welfare services would also be diluted by these foreigners. The net result of this one-sided discussion of immigration is to polarize the electorates further through the creation of prejudice, unease, resentment and, most worryingly, narrow-minded nationalism.

An illustration of this was when the UK decided to hold a referendum to leave the EU in 2016. Membership of the EU, which allows migration and freedom of movement within the EU, was cited by those campaigning to leave (the leavers) as the main, and perhaps even the only, reason to leave the EU. They campaigned solely, and mischievously, on the perceived negatives of the EU, often with deliberate and misleading information about the principle of freedom of movement within the Union. There were even documented attempts by the leavers to use social media and special software applications to illegally obtain private and personal data, thus enabling them to socially profile individuals who could be targeted as potential leavers. These were cynical attempts to bend the truth and distort a meaningful debate on being a member of the EU. In the UK, there has always been a xenophobic, anti-European and thus anti-immigration tendency as a core ideology on the right wing section of its political spectrum. During the referendum debate, the British people were deliberately misled by some misinformation put forward by the leavers. They alleged that it was the immigrants from EU member states who came and swamped the job scene, thus denying the locals access to employment opportunities. The result of this negative campaign by the leavers shocked the nation when a narrow margin of 52% vs 48% voted to leave the EU. Up to then, even among the most hostile of anti-EU leavers and opportunistic politicians, the general prediction had been that the people would vote for the UK to stay within the EU. There have been many post-mortems on such a surprising result. Most analysts agreed that a xenophobic spin was a significant factor.

When the UK finally left the EU in 2021, after five years of hard and often tempestuous negotiations with the EU on the exit terms, the freedom of movement within the EU became closed to the UK. Those who wish to come to the UK have to have a work visa or apply to be an immigrant. The result of this exit does mean the UK government will have sole control of immigration. The irony is that, after five years of bickering and wrangling, by the time the UK finally left the EU in January 2021, even though the migration of people from the EU has dropped, the overall number of immigrants into the UK has not changed significantly, suggesting that there was an overall increase in the immigration of people from outside the EU up to 2019. The figures of 2020 and 2021 would be distorted due to travel restrictions imposed by the pandemic.

Furthermore, when the UK Office for National Statistics (ONS) published its findings in June 2021, it showed that since 2016, which was the year of the referendum, although the number of EU migrants into the UK has dropped substantially, the number of those EU nationals who were already in the UK choosing to stay in the UK by applying for the EU Settlement Scheme (which means that they can stay in the UK after Brexit) had increased significantly. So it is much too soon to draw any significant conclusion on the earlier referendum statements made by those who advocated to leave the EU in 2016, that leaving would stop EU immigration into the UK. The net effect can only be assessed at least until such a time when the pandemic is truly over. Interestingly, the report also pointed out that there was a significant rise in non-EU immigration into the UK.

On the far side of the globe, things have also changed in Hong Kong. From 2021, immigration has once again become a hot topic of conversation. Most people of Hong Kong, myself included, belong to the generation where immigration was neither a new nor unfamiliar concept. This is because, historically, Hong Kong has itself experienced waves of immigration, mainly from China. For a few decades after WW2, especially in the 1950s, 1960s and 1970s, Hong Kong itself was a major destination for immigrants from China. This can be traced back to the formation of the People's Republic of China in 1949, while Hong Kong was then still a British colony. The population in Hong Kong grew from barely over two million in the 1950s to the present level of 7.5 million, with the vast majority of the growth due to immigrants from China.

This story of Hong Kong is quite unique. It is the only colony of the British Empire post-WW2 that instead of being granted independence to be part of the British Commonwealth, was reunited with its motherland China in 1997. So the early population history of Hong Kong, in its short post-WW2 history, can be summed up as a story of immigration. Thus, the small city of Hong Kong has experienced all the ups and downs of movement of people. There have been periods in Hong Kong when people chose to emigrate to other countries. This emigration tended to happen in waves. It often coincided with the periods in Hong Kong when there was widespread concern and misgivings about its political future and uncertainty. Most notably, people wondered in the 1970s and 1980s what life would be like when Hong Kong was to change from being a British-run colony to a city under Chinese sovereignty, with a large degree of autonomy granted by China. Therefore, emigration has always been a matter of active and ongoing social discussion. In the minds of the Hong Kong people, there is almost always a nagging question popping up from time to time: to leave or not to leave, that is the question.

Like immigrants in other places, the people of Hong Kong have similar aspirations. We have always yearned for a home in a settled place. But compared with many cities, Hong Kong does have a significant disadvantage in terms of liveable space. It is a small city of just about 1,000 sq km, so personal living space comes at a huge premium, unaffordable for most. These days, those eligible to apply for government-assisted housing schemes have a minimum waiting time of five years. Back in the early 1970s, the situation was even worse. There were hardly any liveable public housing schemes. I was one of those early emigrants from Hong Kong in the late 1970s in search of a life with more open space!

More recently, there is another wave of emigration from Hong Kong. It started in 2021. Political events and social unrest in Hong Kong over the preceding two years have prompted many in the city once again to rekindle concerns about their future and, more importantly, the future of their children. Thus, emigration has once again raised its head. But this time, the emigration wave is quite unique. Historically, many of the popular destination countries among the Hong Kong Chinese, namely the UK, Canada, Australia and even the USA, had one of the world's harshest immigration policies. The bar to entering these countries was set very high as a way to deter mass applications. But from the early 2020s, these countries have made targeted changes specifically for the Hong Kong people by extending a welcoming hand to those Hongkongers who wish to emigrate. This is a phenomenon which has not been seen since WW2. Prior to this, immigration to these countries was seen by many in Hong Kong as too hard. Moreover, since the handover of Hong Kong to China in 1997, the situation in Hong Kong was by and large very peaceful with almost uninterrupted economic growth and rise in per-capita income, hence emigration and brain drain were not on the radar of most people.

The turning point was June 30, 2020 when China passed a Hong Kong National Security Law to be enshrined in the Basic Law of Hong Kong. This new law was introduced because, since June 2019, Hong Kong went through significant civic disorders with repeated public demonstrations demanding for democracy. There were severe interruptions and outbreaks of violence. It became worldwide front-page news. As a result of this law, things gradually returned to normal, as most of the active protesters were either imprisoned or went abroad. Political protests are no longer allowed. Those who yearn for changes started to worry about their own life and the lives of their children. In view of this, the UK, USA, Canada and Australia started to encourage the people of Hong Kong to emigrate by lowering their bar of entry significantly, making immigration into these countries much easier. The official figures released by the Home Office in the UK showed that in the first two quarters of 2021, since the introduction of the eligibility to enter the UK for Hong Kong citizens who hold the British National Overseas (BNO) status, 65,000 eligible Hongkongers applied to emigrate to the UK, and by September 2021, there were 90,000 applicants.

CHAPTER 3

The general history of migration and immigration

Immigration is not a modern phenomenon, though it had a different meaning in the ancient past. It has a history almost as long as the history of Homo sapiens. In fact, it is very much the story of Homo sapiens. We were all, just like our ancestors, migrants at some stage. The term 'migrant' is not defined under international law, and there is not a commonly accepted definition either. A migrant can be loosely defined as someone who moves away from his or her place of usual residence. Therefore, it can also be used to refer to the free movement of people within a country. Indeed, it has always been explained by the economists that one of the main reasons for the remarkable economic success of China achieved over the last 40 years was the free movement of people (migrants) from the countryside to its newly industrialized cities. In other words, the labour force needed in China was provided by the migrants from within the country.

To try to understand immigration, it is necessary to look at the human desire for movement through the lens of the many thousands of years of human history. In other words, one needs to look at migration first, which predates the modern definition of immigration. The fundamental principle, though, is the same, and which is, those who desire to migrate or immigrate have to be prepared to make a proactive effort to journey into the unknown. In doing so, they also have to be prepared to endure uncertainties, adversities and hardships throughout this journey.

When we trace the metamorphosis of migration to immigration, we can possibly draw the conclusion that migration as a human endeavour can be dated as early as the emergence of Homo sapiens. This was estimated to be dated around a rough period of between 400,000 and 1.5 million years ago. This need for moving around to places further afield, i.e. migration, was based on the survival and primal need of our ancestors in search of better and more stable food supply, a more suitable habitat with a climate conducive for them to change from a nomadic life to a more settled and non-nomadic life very gradually over perhaps hundreds of years. Then this settled life paved the way for the formation of a communal life which in turn would lead to the emergence of a civilized and urban life. In the prehistoric times, it is estimated that our ancestors moved out of Africa into Asia, Near East and Europe some

125,000 years ago. This process of migration involved a great deal of adventurism and exploration. It mainly happened on the known landmass at the time. Movement across oceans, which required vessels and navigation, were developed much later.

Ancient civilizations, by which I mean the formation of a settled community of humans, each given a different but specific role within an organized community, started, by common consent, about 5,000 years ago, in an area around present-day Iraq, along the River Tigris and River Euphrates. Even then, it was estimated that these civilized metropolitan lives only involved around 10% of the population, while the remaining 90% were still living a farm life. This allowed for a great deal of movement from a farm life to a city life. These communities followed roughly the same process of developments, starting as tribes, then metropolises (urban cities), then finally kingdoms, establishing a social structure with the formation of a civic order with rules and regulations. There would be those who ruled and those who were ruled. Migration of people from one region to another was then the norm rather than the exception. Such migration was a fact of life. Then, there were no rules imposed by any societies or kingdoms on how migration could be regulated, if indeed any regulation was thought to be necessary. Quite the contrary, I would imagine; the leaders of tribes and cities would welcome more people to come in to provide more labour. This was why the Romans brought in slaves! So slaves can be seen, quite perversely, as the earliest form of controlled immigration, except that it was forced against the human will. Slaves were owned by their owners, and the origin of where the slaves were from was as unclear as it was unheeded. In modern terms, it was a form of state sponsored but inhuman forced immigration.

Far more common than slaves in our ancient civilization was the free movement, by choice, of people from one place to another, often as a result of escape from wars. Wars, in those years, were fought mainly for territorial expansion. Territorial expansion always resulted in the free movement of people as migration. For instance, Ancient Greece, regarded by many as one of the most advanced civilizations which laid the foundation of Europe, started its territorial expansion some 700 years BCE, peaking at the time of Alexander the Great. Thus an empire was established, which necessitated and encouraged the migration of people from Greece to Africa, Asia, as far as India, and vice versa. The same happened in the Assyrian Empire and the Babylonian Empire too. Human progress in our 5,000 years of history was only made possible by population growth and the accommodation of such a growth, which, in turn, was only made possible by the migration of people.

The history of the Jewish people, famed for their monotheism faith and their remarkable ability to move and adapt, is another classic story of migration and immigration from the ancient times to the modern times. There is a specific word for this unique ability of the Jewish people to settle outside their homeland. It is called diaspora (more on this later when Chinese immigration is discussed). In biblical times, Jewish people moved from their ancient land Canaan (somewhere in the Ancient Near East) to Egypt. Then there was their migration to Eastern Europe, Russia, Western Europe and more recently in the last 200 years, the USA. No other race in the history of the world can be compared with the remarkable ability of the Jewish people throughout their history in embracing emigration and migration. When it comes to the study of migration and immigration, the Jewish people stand out distinctly. The main reason is that the Jewish people did not have their own state since they were in exile during various periods in biblical times, so there was a constant need for them to migrate, and only when the state of Israel was established in 1948 did the Jewish people have a country of their own.

The next key timeline of reference for mass migration is the Black Death, occurring in the Afro-Eurasia world from 1346 to1353. The American continents, though inhabited by native populations, were not known to the world then, so the Afro-Eurasia continental mass could be regarded as the only known world (commonly called the Old World) which was available for human migration on a significant scale. The Black Death devastated this known world. It was estimated to have killed between 75 million and 200 million people. Regardless of the exact death toll, it was a human catastrophe. Indeed, it was the first recorded global catastrophe. It was estimated that over a period of four years, between 45% and 50% of the European population died of the disease. It was thought by some that the Black Death might have originated in China (the popular theory points to the Yuan Dynasty when the Mongols were known for their nomadic lifestyle and their conquest through Asia Minor to Europe) in the early to mid-1300s. The transmission spread, almost unchecked, over a vast landmass, at the height of the East-West land-based trade (the Silk Road started in the Han Dynasty around 130 BCE) stretching from China to Asia Minor, Europe and North Africa.

Although we now know the Black Death refers to the bubonic plague, caused by the bacteria Yersinia pestis and spread by infected fleas from small animals such as ground rodents, this cause of the Black Death was not known then. Since the cause was not known, the fear of catching the disease was such that the only way to avoid it was to move away from areas severely affected by the disease to as far out as possible. As a result, there was a great migration of people from Central Asia westward towards the European continent. Of course, those who migrated could not have possibly foreseen that Europe was by then also suffering from a huge number of deaths as a direct result of the infection. Some historians commented that the migrants were thus helping, inadvertently, to spread the disease. I would guess, in their defence, that had they known that Europe was also badly affected, they would not have migrated. The real culprits of the spread, in modern terms, were: poor sanitation, overcrowding, and the lack of understanding of the disease, especially the transmission of the disease by rodents. Out of fear and ignorance of the disease, migrants moved to escape from it. They would not knowingly or willingly spread the disease, and thus attribution of blame to these migrants seemed to be quite unfair and inappropriate.

If we fast forward a few hundred years from then to look at the Covid-19 pandemic in the 21st century, which is the first pandemic in our lifetime, the picture is vastly different. As soon as it was determined that Covid-19 is a transmissible infection caused by a respiratory virus known as the coronavirus, all countries were advised by the World Health Organization (WHO) to shut down borders. International air travels were severely curtailed. Those who are allowed to travel, immigrants or otherwise, are treated equally by an internationally acceptable standard, namely a negative virus test and often a period of mandatory quarantine on arrival.

Any discussion on immigration cannot be completed without special mention of the USA. The USA, founded in 1776, gained its independence to become a republic from the then colonial British Empire. It was a young country, full of dynamism and optimism, endowed with vast natural resources including the most precious of all, land. But this young country was short of human resources. Over the ensuing 100 years, the USA constantly expanded its territory, with the acquisition of the state of California in 1850 after the US-Mexico War ended. So, the border of this vast country of huge landmass stretches from its east coast facing the Atlantic Ocean to its west coast facing the Pacific Ocean. This expansionist approach, from east to west, was relentless and was a cornerstone of its national policy ever since the founding of the USA. In 1776, there were 13 states, all of which were primarily near the East Coast; and by 2017, there were in total 50 states. Implicit in this expansionist approach is a requirement for massive infrastructure developments, especially on building a vast network of roads and railways to support the agricultural, industrial, commercial and residential needs for the development of new modern cities. Therefore, the USA implemented an open door policy of encouraging and welcoming immigrants from the rest of the world to help in the developments of the country.

At the time, the First Industrial Revolution had just started in Europe. Automation was in its infancy, and robotics was a word not even known then. There was, therefore, a huge demand for human labour for the vast infrastructure work in this New World, which its own resident population was far from adequate to provide. The need for extra labour, especially cheap manual labour, was unprecedented. This proved to be a magnet to attract new immigrants, starting from the middle of the 19th century. There was plenty of work to be done and wages to be earned. As a result of the massive need of immigrants, the USA was then seen as the New World, and prided itself as the Land of Opportunity to attract immigrants from the rest of the world.

The Native Americans and the early settlers from Northern Europe were far from sufficient to develop the full potential of this new country. For instance, cotton, so important to the textile industry, had to be grown and picked by slaves bought and brought over from the African continent and the West Indies. It is often cited by modern historians that the USA, in contrast to many other countries, was founded as a country of immigrants, with Europeans predominantly settling in its east coast, Chinese in its west coast and Latinos in its southern border. It still is regarded by many aspiring immigrants as a Land of Opportunity. No other country can share that accolade. Immigration to the USA was a necessity for the success of the country.

Among this newish generation of immigrants were Jews escaping from the political and economic oppression in tsarist Russia, antisemitism in European countries and then Nazi Germany. There were also Irish, Polish, Hungarians, Czechs, Serbs, Slovaks, Greeks, and even as far eastward as Syrians, Turks and Armenians. The reasons for the massive immigration from the Old World included wars, droughts, famines, and religious and political persecutions. People in Europe looked west and noticed that there was a vast continent across the ocean, where opportunities were abundant. And so they moved, to a new life in the New World.

This is where the story of Ellis Island in New York comes in. Situated right next to the Statue of Liberty in New York Harbor, the island and the statue are revered as the two major iconoclastic landmarks, showcasing what the USA is all about. The Statue of Liberty is a colossal neoclassical sculpture on Liberty Island in the Harbor. This copper statue was a gift from France to the people of the USA in 1886 to celebrate the centenary of the founding of the USA. Right next to the Statue is Ellis Island, which represented a landmark of equal significance to the Statue. Together, right at the centre of New York Harbor, they represent the high ideals of the American spirits – freedom and liberty. And, for all the various domestic problems and internal debates affecting the USA in recent years, it is undeniable that the USA is still by far the only country in the world which is a melting pot that strives for the human spirits of multiculturalism, racial and ethnic openness, tolerance and coexistence.

Ellis Island occupies a key chapter in the annals of immigration in the USA. Its history occupies an indispensable part in the modern discussion of immigration. Ellis Island, located at the mouth of the Hudson River, has a land area of 27.5 acres. It was chosen by the US Federal government as an immigration processing centre. It was opened in 1892 until its closure in 1954. From 1892 to 1924, Ellis Island was America's largest and busiest immigration centre. It was estimated that 12 million immigrants were processed at the Island. In fact, it is also estimated that close to 40% of all current US citizens can trace at least one of their ancestors who came to the USA via Ellis Island.

At the time, the US immigration policy was to process the immigrants on arrival through documentation and health check. An entry visa was granted on site at the point of entry. But very soon, this policy of checking on arrival proved to be ineffective and indeed not fit for purpose. The vast numbers of unpredictable arrivals on a daily basis clearly was intolerable and unmanageable for the host country to cope and process there and then. Documents were often faked, verification impossible, identity often unknown, health could not be ascertained, transmissible diseases often undetected, and the language barriers unsurmountable. Names were often assigned or misspelled. There were chaos, confusion and anxiety affecting both the migrants and the officials. As a result, the US government changed its immigration policy and decided that the application process with verifiable documentation had to be initiated at the home country. Ellis Island was finally closed in 1954 for good. From then on, all immigration applications can only be initiated by the applicants from their home countries where the USA has consular representation.

The significance of Ellis Island, therefore, is that, however welcoming a host country may be for the immigrants, the process must be managed in an organized way. Vetting has to be done properly, and it often takes time. Ellis Island, initially chosen as a processing centre, quickly passed its sell-by date, but its values lie in its symbolism of capturing the spirits of immigration to the New World from people all over Europe. It occupies a uniquely distinctive role in the history of immigration.

These two landmarks, Ellis Island and the Statue of Liberty, are still very popular tourist attractions, not only for overseas visitors, but for Americans too, who are rightly proud to have such physical landmarks representing the American founding spirits of liberty and freedom. Ellis Island is now a museum in recognition of its historic role as the gatekeeper of immigration from Europe to the USA. When I first visited the museum many years ago, I was very moved by what I saw. There were many children on organized school trips to learn of the history of immigration of the USA. I also saw unclaimed personal belongings such as diaries, items of discarded clothing and shoes. There were also black and white photos of poignant human sentiments such as the look of bewildered kids, grown-ups with anxious faces, tearful faces and, most movingly, joyful faces. It gave me a real flavour of how the hopes and aspirations of the immigrants were finely poised while they were detained at Ellis Island.

Ellis Island also sets in motion a more proper and humane way of handling immigration. The policy of applying for immigration at the point of departure of a country and not at the point of entry to the country of destination is now the international standard of all countries which receive immigration. The sixty years of massive, almost uncontrollable immigration at Ellis Island was clearly pivotal in this change of policy initiated by the US government.

I am very fortunate that I can travel to so many places in the world, but I have not come across a set of structures such as the Statue of Liberty and Ellis Island which portray for me so vividly the aspirations and adventurism of the human spirits. Perhaps Robben Island in South Africa comes close.

CHAPTER 4

What is the impact of immigration and why do people immigrate?

There is no international definition or standard of immigration, as each country may have different policies for different classes of immigrants. According to the Oxford Dictionary, the definition is rather simple and therefore incontestable. It means the action of coming to live permanently in a foreign country.

The term immigration was coined first in the 17th century, when sovereign states started to be defined by their territories and borders, especially in the European continent, with each sovereign state (which was also known as kingdom) ruled by a monarch in its own territorial borders. Disputes over territories and borders were often settled by wars between two nation states or, more often, among multiple nation states. Immigration through border control was fairly rudimentary then, in the sense that borders could be easily crossed, for instance, in the darkness of the night or in disguise, without much fear of being caught.

After WW2, more and more countries became independent (193 countries are now registered with the United Nations), each with its own borders. There are no longer any empires such as the Austria Hapsburg Empire, the British Empire or the Ottoman Empire. While there were regional blocs of alliances such as the former Soviet Union, many alliances are now based on signed treaties by sovereign heads of states, without affecting the control of the borders of any countries. Therefore, immigration is now generally regarded as the movement of people from one country to another country, and is subject to approval by the destination country, which is occupied by its own residents typically defined as born natives. Immigrants are by definition not born natives, and thus they do not possess citizenship. However, those who are given an entry visa as immigrants to a destination country would be allowed to settle and to seek work, and after a certain period (in the UK it is five years), they can be accepted as permanent or naturalized citizens with the right of abode.

The word immigrant originated from Latin, and it means 'move or shift'. Emigration refers to the choice of leaving a place, and immigration refers to the permission to enter a country. So for me, I was an emigrant from China, first immigrating to Hong Kong and then becoming an emigrant again from Hong Kong, immigrating to the UK.

The impact of immigration could be discussed by studying the USA. Most historians would agree that the USA was founded on the basis of immigration, even though there were already natives living in the North America continent much earlier before people from Northern Europe arrived. When Christopher Columbus discovered America in 1492, he noted that the indigenous people were of a darker complexion, and so mistakenly but unintentionally, he thought he had reached India, and thus the words Red Indians were used. This was of course a wrong choice of words and these local residents nowadays are properly recognized as Native Americans, as opposed to the white people who were the later settlers coming to North America from Europe followed then by the black people from the African continent and the Caribbean Islands. The black people arrived in the USA as part of a trade in human commodity known as the slave trade. It is not possible to be clear about the size of the population of the Native Americans prior to 1776. It was estimated to vary from a low of 2.1 million to 7 million; some estimated that it could be as high as 18 million! This rough estimation nevertheless suggested a very significant native population. To put this in perspective, a land mass of a fairly equivalent size as North America around the 16th century was the then Ming Dynasty in China, which was at the time the most populous country in the world, with a population of around 60 million in around AD1500 while England then had a population of 3 million. At the founding of the US Republic in 1776, the population (not including the Native Americans) was estimated to be around 2.5 million for the 13 states, which was likely to be made up primarily by the white colonizers from the British Empire and continental Europe. This is to say that the population of the Native Americans could quite possibly be higher than the number of the white settlers from Europe at the time of the US War of Independence. It was clear that these settlers first went to America as immigrants, for reasons not different from immigrants to other places. These early and subsequent generations became so successful and dominant that they then fought and won the War of Independence. It was unfortunate that despite their dominance in shaping and charting their events, the interests of the Native Americans were largely ignored.

By 2020, the population for the whole of the USA was 331 million. Such a population expansion of more than 100-fold clearly could not be explained purely by population growth of the indigenous population and the new settlers. It explicitly means that this remarkable growth was fuelled by a huge and ongoing influx of immigrants, who have collectively made important social, economic, and cultural contributions to the USA over centuries. The USA is a country blessed with abundant natural resources, but it is also blessed by this remarkable population growth through immigration. This is why the USA has always been proud of being the beacon of the world and to this very day, it is still viewed by many as The Land of Opportunity. For decades, the USA has remained by far the most popular destination country for immigration, both from Europe and Asia. In its relatively brief history of just about 250 years, no other country comes close to being comparable to the ability of the USA in absorbing such a scale of inward immigration.

There is a light-hearted anecdote regarding immigration to the USA. In late January 1979, the then paramount leader of China, Deng Xiao Ping, undertook the first ever state visit by a senior Chinese leader to the USA. He was warmly welcomed by US President Carter. It was reported that during one of the light-hearted chats between him and President Carter, the President told Deng that the USA was founded as a country of immigrants and would welcome immigrants from China too, to which Deng replied jokingly that China could send over 10 million Chinese the next day as immigrants! Different interpretations were given for this brief and interesting exchange, but it did somehow reflect that in those days, even before Deng's policy of *gaikekaifeng* (reform and opening up), there was a tacit admission by all that the USA was the country of choice for those in China who might wish to emigrate.

Why do people emigrate? Conventional wisdom suggests that the main reason people migrate is that they yearn for a better life, often to escape from poverty or poor employment opportunities. However, my own view of immigration is that this is only part of the story. Certainly, in the 20th century and the first two decades of the 21st century, there are other reasons. For many modern-day immigrants, the aim is not necessarily a better or more prosperous life. Indeed, many immigrants nowadays already have reasonably comfortable lives in their own countries, often they are middle-class professionals. They emigrate because they may want a different life and different lifestyle. Many also emigrate out of consideration for the educational needs of their children.

Take Hong Kong, for example. Hong Kong is an international and prosperous city. It enjoys a very modern mix of public and private education systems, with plenty of international schools in the private sector. These are schools not under the control of the Education Department of the Hong Kong SAR government. These international schools are run independently, with a syllabus based on the educational standards in the English-speaking countries in the West, especially the USA and UK. These schools were originally set up to cater for the educational needs of the children of expatriates sent to work in Hong Kong by the multinational companies. The idea was to seamlessly enable these children to enter tertiary education abroad, mainly in the USA. These schools are now very popular in Hong Kong, and in fact, a vast majority of the pupils in these schools are children of Hong Kong residents, since many of them feel the public education system has too intense a curriculum with excessive homework imposed on the pupils. Furthermore, in recent years, the Education Department in Hong Kong decided to modify its core educational curriculum by placing more emphasis on the modern history of China. This was because it was long thought by some that this aspect of history was not adequately taught in Hong Kong and, indeed, was seen by many to be one of the root causes of the social unrest which swept Hong Kong in June 2019. As a result of the curriculum changes, many Hong Kong middle-class parents with young families have chosen to emigrate with their children. These parents wish to provide for their children a different system of education based on a balanced and all-round curriculum, which is less demanding in nature. This education principle is very much the standard in the West, which is that children can best be educated not purely through the tools of rote learning, private tuition and competition in examinations. The main role of the school is to help each student to reach his/her own ceiling, not at a rushed-off-the-feet pace, but rather at an individually adjusted pace.

There is another class of immigrants, which is a relatively modern phenomenon, especially noted in the wealthy countries in the West. The name of this type of immigrants is most interesting, reflecting a kind of political reality and acceptance that money does help to buy influence or access. These people are not called immigrants. Instead, they have a much grander name to reflect their status. This new class of people can sort of, legally speaking, 'buy' their way into becoming an accepted immigrant much more speedily in their chosen destination country. The entry requirement is often based on their net wealth, and it varies from country to country, but the general principle of wealth being used as a shortcut is much the same. This trend became far more noticeable since the end of the Cold War, when after the dissolution of the Soviet Union, many people with financial means from the former Soviet Union decided to move to Europe, the UK or the USA.

In the UK, the Home Office labels this as Tier 1 Investor Visa (a very attractive name which may appeal to the vanity of the rich), which requires an investment of GBP 2 million. This scheme was introduced in 2008, the same year as the last global financial crisis. It is called investment, but in fact, anyone with a bank account of such an amount (aka rich individuals with high net worth) can be seen as bringing investment to the UK by simply depositing the required amount in a UK bank. In other words, they are investing in the UK banking industry. To be fair, the basic desires of these people are no different from the other immigrants. They both move because they want a different life. The only difference is that these investors are so rich that they do not have to work for a living and cannot be viewed, in any shape or form, as a drain on the welfare state. They come to the UK to spend, and not to earn, so often they pay little tax too. This is perfectly legal. The massive influx of such wealthy people who come with Tier 1 Investor Visa is the main reason why the property prices in London have skyrocketed in recent years to a level beyond the reach of most local Londoners, who work and pay their taxes in the UK. The political reason often used in welcoming these investors was that they brought in wealth to boost up the local economy by providing new employment opportunities for the local people such as cleaners, personal childminders, security guards and chauffeurs. Whether they actually enrich the life and culture in the destination country is a different matter for discussion and debate.

More recently, as the world evolves in the 21st century towards more globalization, hyper-connectivity, digitalization and knowledge-based economy, there is another group of immigrants who are also very welcomed by the host countries, not for their wealth but for their unique skill set. These are the professional classes consisting of people such as IT engineers, software developers, data analysts, fintech experts, academics, and those in the advanced medical fields especially biotechnologists. By all accounts, these people are needed in any country they choose to move to. Their skill is globally applicable and transcends any national boundaries.

CHAPTER 5

Debates on immigration – two sides of the coin

After WW2, the world split into two major geopolitical blocs. Countries began to separate into spheres of capitalism and communism. The term First World was termed by the United Nations in the late 1940s. Today, this term is slightly out of date and is seldom used. It has no official definition. Nevertheless, it generally refers to the capitalist, industrial, wealthy and developed countries which are also popular destination counties for immigrants. As such, immigration has always been, and will remain, a very sensitive issue which is hotly debated in the formulation of national policy in these countries. It requires a need of these rich countries to have workable and acceptable (to the natives) policy on immigration. There is also a constant need for revisions and updates of such policy to reflect the prevalent social trends, population profile, developments and progress in any given society at any given time, thus enabling better integration of an acceptable level of immigrants in these countries.

Although immigration appears to be, at least in theory, a binary problem involving two sides (the host country and the immigrants), the factors involved in this are extremely complex, generating strong and even controversial sentiments. For a start, it is very unidirectional, as immigrants tend less to move back to where they came from. The onus therefore very much falls on the country of destination to accept and accommodate them. This involves a complex interplay and consideration of a country's national heritage, culture, economic needs and the skill set of its native labour force in a modern society. In addition, the host country also has to assess the impact of any extra demands on services such as housing, education, medical and social provisions. A workable and successful immigration policy must be based on these considerations at a national level. Equally, those who are planning to become immigrants should only make a decision based on their own individual assessment and preferences, and choose a host country into which they could assimilate.

In recent years, the sensitive and divisive opinions on matters regarding immigration can best be illustrated by the Brexit story in the UK. Most political scientists and commentators accepted that immigration was one of the reasons for the exit of the UK from the European Union. The referendum in the UK was held in June 2016. The main argument, put forward by the 'leavers', was that it enables the UK to 'take back control', by which it means sovereignty, mainly in the control of immigration. In other words, the UK wished to be excluded from the key principles of the EU, which state that within the EU, there will be freedom of movement of people, employment, goods, services and capital among all its member states. During the EU referendum campaign in the UK in 2016, the anti-immigration card was very cleverly, though completely immorally, played and exploited politically by those who advocated leaving the EU. At the height of the debate, truth became untruth and repeated lies became perceived facts. An impression was created that the UK would be swamped by uncontrolled immigrants arriving from all over the EU. The controversies and the political problems dragged on, even after the referendum result was to leave the UK. It was not until five years later, in 2021, that the UK finally exited from the EU.

Up to the early 21st century, as difficult and controversial as they were, the debates on immigration were mainly focused on its economic and social impact. However, the emergence of social platforms allows for the fast and instantaneous messages and opinions to be instantly available at the tap of a button on any mobile devices. Thus, subjective, negative and unchecked opinions on an issue such as immigration can be easily expressed and, worse still, quickly disseminated on Twitter, Instagram or TikTok etc. In addition, the already emotional issue of immigration is further complicated by new social trends such as debates on identity crisis, LGBT (lesbian, gay, bisexual and transgender) and the WOKE (an awareness of sensitive social issues) cultures. When these new social discussions are all thrown into the mix of discussion on immigration, the field will be much more crowded, complicated, and the tone more disagreeable and even nastier. Scholars, economists, political scientists, social commentators are all acutely aware of the complex interplay here and indeed have discussed these at length, but fail to reach any consensus. The arguments on these are, regrettably, so circular in nature. For instance, nobody really knows what the exact nature of identity politics is, as it depends very much on what identity it is referring to. This identity can vary from the traditional religious, cultural and ethnic identity to the more modern sexual identity, dietary identity and even generational identity. Yet, the use of such words has increased exponentially in the media. The boundaries between truth and falsehood, honesty and lying are blurred deliberately and consistently, and are replaced by artful and manipulative spinning, leaks and fake news. Post-truth politics has become the standard tool of populist politics. One can easily get a fair appreciation of this by simply watching any election or political campaign, where soundbites and post-truth politics have completely displaced sensible debates on policy rationale.

So, against this background, rational discussion on immigration is becoming very difficult. A cool, detached and impartial discussion on immigration is guaranteed to be a vote loser in any political popularity contests. For every protagonist for immigration, one can be sure that there are many more antagonists, especially among the politicians. Politicians are supposed to advise and lead, but often they inflame.

Since the end of WW2, the world has enjoyed uninterrupted peace, apart from regional conflicts and wars. As a result of this peace dividend, countries (especially those in the West collectively known as liberal democracies) have become richer and richer, and standards of living higher and higher. The increase in prosperity is one of the main reasons why immigration from the poorer countries to the rich countries has expanded hugely. It is now a global trend, on a scale that never could have been foreseen in the immediate post-WW2 period. Adding to this, the convenience of modern communications, such as telecommunication and affordable air travel, helps to ensure that homesickness has become much less of an issue of concern for those who emigrate. For instance, for someone like me, I can stay connected with others without having to leave my house, as long as I am tuned in to the world of cyberspace or, if I choose, can fly back to where I came from to see friends and families, without much restriction, apart from the time plus the cost of an airline ticket.

As we move out of the teenage years of the 21st century, the world has become post-colonial. No one talks about colonies anymore. Yet, the footprints of the colonial period are still very much in existence. In general, the people in previous colonies tended to migrate to their colonial master country. For example, those from Indonesia may wish to move to the Netherlands, those from India (the Jewel of the Crown of the

British Empire) to the UK, and those from African countries such as Algeria, Tunisia and Morocco to France. When these people move, they quite reasonably bring with them their own cultural heritage, i.e. their own identity. This is entirely understandable, but it does pose a further potential challenge to the attainment of a cultural equilibrium in the destination country.

Notwithstanding these difficulties, it is still important to explore how, in this 2020s era, the issue of immigration can be debated. We need to have a fresher look and come up with information to properly appraise the matter, so the public can be better informed and thus better prepared, the governments can be better positioned, and expectations from both sides can be better managed. To understand a problem is a prerequisite to solving the problem.

Traditionally, the debates on the pros and cons of immigration tend to focus mainly along two lines. The protagonists tend to focus on the economic benefits, while the antagonists tend to focus on the negative side of immigration as a cause of social disharmony, resentment and even hatred. The presence of social media makes the negative side much more appealing, as exuberant negativity can be more easily translated into soundbites compared with rational persuasion.

These two lines of argument are especially intense in countries such as the USA, the EU, the UK, Canada and Australia. All of these countries, except those in the EU, are English-speaking. All these countries, including the EU, have a native population which is predominantly white Caucasians. Some would call them the Anglo-Saxon world and the European world. If immigration is not handled properly, then it could give rise to resentment, leading to overt racism and challenges to law and order. Insidiously, this path will lead to the people becoming radicalized and even weaponized. Social harmony, a key core value for humanities, will be eroded, leading to the fracturing and disintegration of social cohesion. One of the key reasons why the UK electorate chose to vote Leave in its national referendum on its position in the EU in 2016 was precisely because those politicians on the Leave side played the emotional card of immigration. In the case of the UK, the electorate voted, by a margin of 52% to 48%, to leave the EU and thus rejected the principle of unchecked freedom of movement and employment within the EU. Little was mentioned of the fact that the main reason for the apparent natural choice of many people to the UK, especially those from eastern EU countries, was simply because they could speak English better than they could speak French, German or Spanish. They did not choose to come to the UK because they thought the UK was easy on immigration.

For the protagonists of immigration, a key and powerful argument put forward is on the economic impact of immigration. For example, according to the UK government HMRC (Her Majesty's Revenue and Customs), in the financial year 2015/16 (the year before the UK referendum), EEA (European Economic Area, which covers countries in the EU plus Iceland, Norway and Liechtenstein) nationals paid £15.5 billion more in income tax than they took out in tax credits and child benefits. A study by Oxford Economics in 2018 (two years after the referendum to leave the EU) showed that recent migrants from the EEA offered the biggest fiscal benefit (+ £4.7 billion), while non-EEA migrants offered a small fiscal drag (- £9 billion) with the UK-born residents bearing the biggest net tax burden (- £41 billion).

In a more recent report published in early 2022 by the UK Office of National Statistics (ONS), it showed a projection that by the end of this decade, there will be an estimated 5.6 million long-term immigrants into the UK and an estimated 3.4 million long-term emigrants from the UK while 6.6 million people will be born and 6.7 million people will die. As such, there will be a net gain of population, mainly made up by long-term immigrants, of about 2.2 million. Using this information, the Financial Times (FT) in the UK calculated, based on additional figures supplied by the Office of Budget Responsibility on the differences in taxes paid and public expenditure, that the UK government will need to find £35 billion in tax revenue each year, rather than the £145 billion as originally predicted by the ONS forecast made in 2014. The FT concluded, therefore, that this population change provides the UK with an unexpected boost to public finances, with the main improvement being predicated on the arrival of new long-term immigrants.

This will provide a strong and affirmative argument against the notion that immigration will drain the local economy because of the extra social welfare costs. In the modern age, immigration provides the most precious of all resources, the human resource. It brings net economic benefits to the host country by providing an additional labour force which is young and almost certainly more flexible, as immigrants tend to be less choosy with job opportunities.

It is my view also that with the new wave of immigrants from Hong Kong in 2021, there would be further net fiscal gain for the UK Treasury. The underlying reasons why this should be so are not difficult to ascertain. These immigrants tend to be younger. They are joining a workforce in a society with an ageing population. According to the Times of London in the UK, about 90,000 immigrants from Hong Kong were granted UK entry in the first nine months of 2021. Figures quoted in the Economist showed that the median age of these immigrants was 37, with more than two-thirds being university educated, and the majority married with children. Many came with a professional background, especially those related to health services such as doctors, nurses, therapists, radiographers and pharmacists. Thus, they can help to ease the current skill shortages, unambiguously exposed in the UK National Health Service by Covid-19. Furthermore, most of these nouveau immigrants from Hong Kong came well prepared with independent financial means and as such they are far less likely to exert a downward drain on the welfare state.

The antagonists of immigration will use, ironically, economic arguments of a different kind. They point out that this enlarged labour pool will have a potential negative impact on real wages. As more people are now coming to share the same pie, so each will get a smaller portion of the pie. Of course, they are missing the point here. The aim of the economy of any country is growth, which means a bigger pie. This bigger pie for sharing will mean that the overall prosperity is increased, and it would help to enhance the overall competitiveness for any country in this knowledge-based global market.

The antagonists also persistently pointed out, with no real solid and verifiable data to back up their claims, that immigration will drain and divert resources for services for local people such as housing, medical and educational needs. These claims are unfounded. I can certainly speak for the medical services. From my personal experience of being a hospital doctor in the NHS for more than 30 years, I have yet to witness any evidence or situations where hospital services provision for the local population is adversely affected to any degree by the presence of immigrants. To my knowledge, no data has been published on this either.

In a King's Fund (a well-respected independent think tank involved with work relating to the health system in England) report, published in 2015, on the impact of immigration on the NHS, it drew the conclusion that the extent to which immigrants and visitors make use of the NHS services is difficult to determine. This report also pointed out that the average use of health services by immigrants and visitors appears to be lower than that of people born in the UK. It further noticed that immigrants do actually make up a substantial part of the NHS workforce. More recent figures according to information from the UK Parliament published in 2021 showed that 14.6 % of the 1.3 million staff in the NHS have a non-British nationality.

Quite apart from the usual discussions on the pros and cons of immigration mentioned above, which most readers would have been familiar with, there are two other areas of sensitive discussions, which for me are far more disturbing. One is Social Darwinism and the other is the White Man's Burden, both of which would steer discussion of immigration from a humanitarian and socio-economic angle to one which borders on racism, bigotry, and inequality. These, therefore, are worthy of further elaboration.

The first is the concept of social Darwinism, proposed by the English philosopher Herbert Spencer in the late 1800s, after the First Industrial Revolution, when the then modern and enlightened world was regarded as located primarily in Europe and the USA. Social Darwinism is a term scholars used to describe the practice of applying the biological theory of Charles Darwin, also an Englishman, to politics, economy and society. Charles Darwin's groundbreaking Theory of Natural Selection (also known as The Theory of Evolution) was published in 1859. His book, On the Origin of Species, is still held universally as one of the greatest books on natural science. It dealt with the biological theory of natural selection of species, evolution and survival of the fittest. The fittest here does not mean the strongest or the most powerful, but rather the fittest to adapt to a changing environment. However, many subsequent scholars and philosophers, who were the proponents of social Darwinists, hijacked and extrapolated this great theory to rationalize the exploitation of one human race by another. In fact, survival of the fittest certainly does not mean survival of the strongest or the presence of a dominant race. Rather, fittest here means those who are best equipped and endowed with the ability to adapt in any biological environment over generations. Darwin used the term species in which humans all belong to one biological species, but Herbert Spencer, in coming up with social Darwinism, regarded humans (Homo sapiens) not as a species but rather different species based on factors such as skin colour and intelligence. So, survival of the fittest would mean the repulsive notion that such survival of the human species does not mean all those in the human race, but rather survival will depend on race and intelligence of a specific race within the same species. They argued that some groups will evolve genetically to become winners and are therefore more superior, while other groups within the same human species will become losers and thus extinct. According to the social Darwinists, any policies that interfere with human competition are detrimental, as they will deprive the gifted and superior social group of its Darwinian advantage. Not surprisingly, many of the social Darwinists also embraced laissez-faire capitalism and racism. They believed the government should not interfere in the 'survival of the fittest' by helping the poor, and promoted the idea that some races are biologically superior to others. This is clearly hubris. Although social Darwinism is now primarily discredited in the 21st century, it nevertheless had a profound impact in the late 19th century. It is entirely conceivable that this social Darwinism theory may have had a profound influence on the enactment of the Chinese Exclusion Act established in1882 as a United States federal law, prohibiting all immigration of Chinese. The Act was repealed later in1943.

The White Man's Burden was originally a political poem written in 1899 by Rudyard Kipling, another Englishman. It is perhaps not wrong to speculate that all these men were English because that was during the height of the British Empire, a time when all these philosophers would take a very English-centric view of the world. The glory of this Empire came with its tribulations too. The historical background to this poem was the Philippine-American War (1899-1902); Kipling was a pro-imperialist poet and wrote the poem to implore the Americans to fight the war and to justify conquests and the creation of an empire as a mission for civilization, which was ideologically related to the expansion philosophy of an imperial destiny of the 19th century. In layman's terms, it means that the white man should bear the burden of armed conflict with a view to conquering and colonizing the inferior, coloured race. That is the only way of introducing civilization to these inferior and colonized people. In the views of those who conquer, their civilization is the only one worth having. So it is their duty, dressed as a burden to provide legitimacy to conquer, to colonize and in so doing, introduce the western civilization as the gold standard of all civilizations. In other words, a form of blatant and naked racism where imperial conquest is dressed up as necessary for the progress of humanities with the concept of white supremacy at its core.

These two views, first surfaced to justify the existence and expansion of empires by the Europeans, are anti-humanitarian in nature but are frequently exploited by the right-wing politicians as a justification against immigration. These views breed perpetual resentment, hatred and prejudice. They are covertly encouraging racism and eugenics. Given that mass immigration is a relatively modern social trend only in the last 200 years, when European powers were at their peak, it is difficult not to conclude that these views formed a formidable hurdle to overcome for the immigrants in the 19th and the early 20th centuries.

As a sign of human progress, since WW2 ended and the formation of the United Nations, where states are recognized and colonies are a thing of the past, nearly all the popular countries of destination for immigrants have made racism, religious bigotry and eugenics illegal. These are now accepted as universal standards for core human values. The twin negative influences of Social Darwinism and the White Man's Burden, though still secretly whispered by some in the far-right sector of the political spectrum, have not entered into any mainstream of policy discussion and debates. The absence of any empire and colonies will help to ensure that the evil of ethnic superiority does not raise its head again to be of any significance worthy of further debate.

CHAPTER 6

The trends of immigration

In my opinion, there are four main types of legal immigration.

The first type is that people move from a poorer country to a richer country. The second type is that people move from a more autocratic country to a more democratic country, unless the autocratic country closes its borders to people who wish to leave. For these two types, hardly anyone moves in the reverse direction. These two types are also the most talked about and easy to understand. The third type is people who move to seek self-enrichment, such as those who move from rich countries to poorer countries to devote themselves to charitable work or missionary work, or those professionals who may wish to try to ply their trade by working in a different country. This type of immigrants can indeed move back to their home country. Of course, the third type is relatively uncommon, compared with the first two types, but nonetheless it does happen. I count myself, having chosen to move from Hong Kong to the UK at a young age, as belonging to this third type. More on this later in Chapter 7. The fourth type is the proactive effort by a host country to attract immigrants.

Based on the above propositions, one can start to assess the general trends in immigration in modern times.

The OECD (Organization for Economic Co-operation and Development), long regarded as an exclusive club representing the richest countries in the world, published in 2021 a comprehensive report on the proportion of foreign-born nationals in various countries. For the USA and the UK, the data collected between 2017 and 2019 showed that the proportion of foreign-born nationals was about 14%, while for Canada it was 21%, and for Australia it was a staggering 30%! It also showed that the top ten destinations for immigration were all industrialized countries in the West with advanced economy. Furthermore, this report revealed that all the 16 countries listed in the report as countries of destination were regarded as democracies, defined as that the leaderships are chosen by an electoral process through universal suffrage.

In a separate report published in January 2020 by the World Economic Forum, it stated that in a period of 24 years from 1995 to 2019, the number of international migrants had increased from 174 million to 272 million, a growth of almost 70%, accounting for about 3.5% of the total world population.

The USA occupied the top spot with a 50 million migrant population. Of the remaining nine countries of destination in the top 10, eight are regarded as countries with high per capita income and these are Germany, the UK, France, Italy, Canada, Australia, Saudi Arabia and the United Arab Emirates.

The Syrian migrant crisis in 2017, as a result of its civil war, led to about 3.7 million migrant people seeking resettlement. This was a humanitarian crisis. The UN played a coordinating role and Turkey ended up taking most of these migrants. Europe, especially Germany, was also heavily involved in resettling these migrants. Even though this crisis involving many undocumented migrants (mainly refugees) is not the remit of this book, it needs to be pointed out that as a result, immigration had once again raised the temperature of political debates within the EU and the wider world. Gallup conducted a survey to assess the scale of the migration trend between 2015 and 2017. According to the findings of the survey published in 2018, a staggering 15% of the world's adults, equating to more than 750 million people, would wish to migrate to another country. Again, of the top 10 countries listed as the choice of destination in this survey, nearly a quarter of those surveyed chose the USA, while both Canada and Germany came second at 6%. All the top 10 countries are regarded as countries with high per capita income. The system of governance in nine of the 10 countries is based on democracy, while the remaining one is based on monarchy rule (Saudi Arabia). Furthermore, these countries are geographically spread across America, Europe, Australasia, and the oil states in the Persian Gulf.

The above findings of OECD, World Economic Forum and Gallup have provided the basic information about immigration trends in the 21st century and validated the first two main trends in immigration which I stated at the beginning of this chapter – that people in general move from a poor to a rich and from a non-democratic to a democratic country.

It is perhaps of some interest for me to add a footnote to this information. Although the USA was the most popular destination country for migration, the top spot for number of foreigners per 100 inhabitants (local population), which is a measure of the density of the migrant population, was Switzerland, followed by Germany, while the UK came in the middle and the USA was not even in the top 10 but came 11th. It meant that the long history of immigration to destination countries such as the USA and the UK (the legacy of the British Empire) has led to the fact that many of the second generation of the immigrants are local born and would therefore no longer be registered as immigrants. It also reflects that the indigenous population of the USA and the UK would have a wider ethnic profile with a richer and more diversified culture through their historical immigration trend and the success of assimilation reflecting a multicultural society. On the other hand, some may argue that this may also explain a tightening up of immigration policy in the USA and the UK in recent years, for fear of the loss of dominance by the non-Caucasian population. Personally, I favour the former view, that enrichment of a society brought about by an emerging diversified culture and ethnicity is much more preferable in this global village to racial or ethnic dominance. It signifies human progress. A diversified culture in a country is an enabler for the country to take a wider world view. It gives all of us a better chance to deal with common global problems such as diseases, pollution, and climate change.

As I mentioned at the beginning of this chapter, there is a fourth trend for immigrants which I, for lack of a better word, would label as targeted immigration. Those being targeted are generally regarded as belonging to the professional skilled middle class. Every country will always, at various stages of its economic and social developments, need a certain type of people to contribute to its progress, but in the process it notices that certain skills to be provided by its own people are found wanting. In other words, the prevailing skill profile of the local workforce may not meet the needs of the country. Hence, one of the ways to fill this 'skill gap' is by attracting specific immigrants with the required skills. Traditionally, this skill gap classically involves the medical services, such as doctors, nurses, therapists, pharmacists or laboratory technicians, where the demands of medical developments far outpace the provision of the necessary skills and expertise. Furthermore, home-grown training required for these skills often takes a long time, not to mention the cost. I myself was lucky enough to be seen as one of these skilled workers when I moved to the UK all those years ago. However, there are other skill gaps too. Globalization and digitalization bring out another type of skill premium required in the present world, and these are the IT people, such as computing engineers, software developers and data analysts. Often, for these skilled professionals, their employers, such as the NHS or global multinational banks and IT conglomerates, will provide them with a sort of sponsorship scheme to fast track the application for entry visas to a country. In fact, these uniquely skilled professionals are needed and welcome in most countries, as their skill base is truly universally suitable, anywhere in the world.

Quite apart from the professional middle class, the skill gap can involve manual workers too. Many countries with an advanced economy are beginning to notice that they are short of skilled manual labour. In this age of automation, robotics and artificial intelligence, we may be forgiven for thinking that society may need less manual labour. We also have a tendency to view many manual tasks as too mundane and too repetitive. We hope that our ever-soaring faith in technology can do all that. Well, we are very wrong. Manual workers, such as painters, decorators, strawberry pickers, domestic helpers, security guards, lorry drivers and plumbers, are always needed, more so in the rich countries. It is worth pointing out that the reason why Saudi Arabia, mentioned in the Gallup survey previously, is popular among migrants is the massive and ongoing infrastructure development programmes that the country has been embarking on. Because it is a rich country, the wage it offers is attractive to migrant workers from the nearby countries in South Asia.

Many countries are beginning to recognize such skill gaps. So they are now modifying their immigration policy by operating a quota and scoring system to control the number of incoming immigrants. The principle is to grade the needs of the country to be matched by its immigration policy. In other words, tasking immigrants to provide a flexible labour force to plug the holes in the provision of a complete skill set required in a modern society. Therefore, the skills which are specially required can be more transparent, in the sense that those who can fill the gaps can score higher in the quota system. This also enables the would-be migrants to check if their own skills on offer can fit into the needs of the destination country. If they do match, then the immigrants can find it easier to enter the country through the granting of an entry visa. A pragmatic and responsive immigration policy such as setting a bar for entry to reflect the needs of the country and match it against the aspirations of the migrants is essential. A most recent failure for such pragmatism can be seen in the case of the UK, following Brexit in 2021. More on this later.

The Covid-19 pandemic has demonstrated, in a most unambiguous manner, our dependence on essential workers such as lorry drivers, delivery men and even seasonal farmworkers in the fields, such as strawberry pickers. We can order the items we want on the internet, but without delivery, we will never receive them. The social commentators and the economists have all agreed that perhaps over-reliance on globalization over the years has an unforeseen downside and Covid-19 has exposed in most countries a lack of strategic resilience. Our obsession with our absolute faith in a seamless globalized supply chain is caught off guard. Nearly all countries were in chaos at the beginning of Covid-19.

Examples of why manual labour is very much still required have been shown during the Covid pandemic in Hong Kong and the situation in the UK following Brexit.

Hong Kong, being an international city of high finance, commerce and trade, has one of the toughest quarantine policies during the Covid pandemic. It has closed its borders to foreign travellers and imposed a mandatory quarantine of 21 days (with the first seven days in a purpose-built quarantine camp). There are few exemptions to these very tough rules and yet the government offers exemptions to lorry drivers who drive across the border to China, for the very basic reason that these lorry drivers are key to the logistics chain for the supply of food and other daily essentials that Hong Kong needs. This is not unique to Hong Kong, either. Many countries classify logistics drivers as essential workers too. In the UK, shortly after Brexit in 2021 and, despite five years of preparation, it found itself grossly short of lorry drivers too. The UK has historically been quite dependent on lorry drivers from the EU to deliver all sorts of goods in both directions. Then, all of a sudden, these drivers and the companies that employed them were asked to fill in form after form for the cross-border transport of goods. The bureaucracy burden led directly to temporary but worrying shortages of petrol and other essential supplies of goods. Unbelievably, there were even shortages of cheap medicine such as paracetamol tablets at some stage and snacks such as potato crisps! The irony is that it was not a true shortage of the goods, but a failure to deliver the goods. So some people turned to the famous e-commerce giant Amazon

UK, and goods got delivered for the simple reason that Amazon was able to increase its profits by selling more goods and paying higher wages to their drivers. In other words, Amazon saw it coming and was able to take quick advantage of the market situation. Apparently, Amazon was equally successful using the same model of practice in the USA too. Belatedly, the UK government recognized lorry drivers as essential workers and went about not only to increase their wages, but actually shorten the period of training for them to obtain the necessary licence. Quite ironically, the government has also fast-tracked applications from those drivers who wish to come to the UK from the EU, barely a year since its exit!

Therefore, it is important for a country to put the sentiments of immigration aside and to predict, prepare, and implement a fit-for-purpose immigration policy to help with the specific needs of the country. To be fit-for-purpose, such a policy must have a tangible long-term plan to deal with the social, welfare, educational and medical needs of the immigrants in a way which can prove acceptable to the local residents, affordable by the government, and reassuring to the immigrants. In my view, the formulation of a long-term and workable policy is mandatory as short-term fixes can be reflected as short-sightedness, opportunistic or last-minute panic, and thus of no real benefit to society.

CHAPTER 7

Emigration from China
in the 19th Century

Historically, emigration from China is fairly well recorded, much like the Jewish history of diaspora. But, unlike the Jewish history in which migration and diaspora have been an ongoing phenomenon throughout the ages, the migration of Chinese overseas tended to be very sporadic in the early years.

In the glorious days of imperial dynastic history of China, such as during the Qin Dynasty, the Han Dynasty and the Tang Dynasty, the migration of people was sea-based or land-based. It was usually done for a specific purpose for the ruling emperor. For instance, during the reign of Qin Shi Huang (the first emperor of the Qin Dynasty 221-210 BCE), he sent people abroad in search of the elixirs of immortality. It was reputed that these people went to and settled in Japan.

In the Han Dynasty (202 BCE-220 AD), migration and settlers tended to be moving westwards for the purpose of territorial expansion and trade interaction with those civilizations to the west of China. This route was later famously known as the Silk Road.

In the Tang Dynasty (618-907 AD), the Silk Road for trade started in earnest, with Tang settlers thought to have resided near Rivers Tigris and Euphrates (present day Iraq). After that, migrants started to move to Southeast Asia (the Chinese named this region Nanyang, meaning Ocean in the South).

Then the Ming Dynasty (1368-1644 AD) came along. The Ming Dynasty was quite unique in the annals of China's imperial history, as it was the first dynasty which was very advanced for its seafaring prowess. The eunuch Cheng He was famous in Chinese history for undertaking no fewer than seven oceanic voyages, reaching as far as the African continent between 1405 and 1433, some 60 years before Christopher Columbus first sailed across the Atlantic Ocean to reach the American continent. His fleet of ships was huge, often multi-masted, weighing 2,000 tons, and carried between 500 and 1,000 passengers. So, unlike the Silk Road, where Chinese could migrate westwards on land, Cheng He's voyages paved the way for Chinese to migrate south and southwest through sea routes.

Up until then, it can be reasonably assumed that the main reasons for the Chinese to migrate were a combination of the need for searching for a particular product and the expansion of trade, through spirits of exploration or adventurism. These migrations were mostly sporadic in nature and never massive in scale.

Then things changed in the 19th and early 20th centuries, when China was riddled with poverty, famines, and foreign invasion from Japan and other European powers. Up until then, the history of invasion of China was mainly from land along its long and tortuous northern land border (hence the building of the Great Wall of China). There were also constant civil wars and power struggles, which finally resulted in a united China following the founding of the People's Republic of China in 1949.

During the long, difficult and humiliating years (between 1842, the Opium War being the historic landmark, and 1949) in Chinese history, migration developed into a trend. It was seen by people as a viable, though full of uncertainties and dangers, escape route which was appealing, especially to those from the densely populated eastern and southern coastal regions such as Fujian and Guangdong provinces. The main reasons why the people chose to migrate were insecurity, unemployment, poverty, starvation and lack of opportunity. These migrants had a desperate wish to build a new life, however far it might be from home, a life which could at least give them some hope of sending repatriations to help their folks who were poverty-stricken at home. They moved either across the Pacific Ocean (a very hazardous journey) to the USA, or to nearby Southeast

Asian countries (less hazardous) like Indonesia, Malaya, Thailand and the Philippines.

Among all these countries, the USA was a big magnet for them and was by far the most popular destination. The early Chinese migrants were told, mainly through hearsay, that the USA was a land full of opportunities and therefore offered untapped riches. In fact, the name of San Francisco, which was often their first port of arrival, was known among the old Chinese migrants as the Old Gold Mountain, and the famous San Francisco Bridge was known to them as the Gold Mountain Big Bridge. News of a gold rush into California was perceived by them that the USA was full of gold, if only they could get there.

The reality, though, was different. Nearly all the immigrants from China into the West Coast of the USA were poorly educated, some were illiterate, and hardly anyone could speak a word of English. So, only hard, unskilled manual labour was what they had to offer. Sadly, for them, it meant they could only do the hardest and most demanding of manual jobs. These jobs would include the building of railways, often involving the excavation of tunnels through mountains, where explosion was regularly part of the building process. Furthermore, their very low social status led to discrimination. Even though they were providing cheap labour of a kind that other jobseekers would refuse, many still blamed the Chinese for a downward pull on workers' wages. They did not have even basic workers' rights for the barest of protection. Many local people, mainly white explorers coming to the West, resented them. The US government therefore enacted the Chinese Exclusion Act of 1882 suspending Chinese immigration for 10 years and declared Chinese immigrants ineligible for naturalization. This was the first significant law restricting immigration by targeting a certain race, despite the fact that the Chinese as a whole composed only 0.002% of the population in the USA. Some historians have put forward the views that this Act was enacted with a political purpose of maintaining white 'racial purity'. Ironically, just over 100 years later, the State of California on the West Coast becomes the most technologically advanced, ethnically diversified, culturally rich and prosperous state in the USA. In the 2020 US census, California was the state with the highest resident population in the country, with 39.5 million people. It also became the first state in the continental US to have a non-white majority, if the Hispanic whites were excluded.

The stories of the Chinese migrants to the USA were indeed full of blood, sweat and tears. They were disadvantaged by their lack of education. They were unable to speak English, so their work was mainly restricted to performing hard labour which did not require much communication, often under conditions which would be illegal by modern standards. It is well documented that even physical punishments such as caning were used for any unsatisfactory performance in the constructions of railways. Thus, they were often treated as slaves. Other Chinese migrants chose work which also did not require language skills, such as laundries or working in kitchens with no breaks. Sick leave was not only unpaid but ignored too. Yet they soldiered on, bearing this hardship with gritted teeth, as their sole intentions were either to repatriate their hard-earned cash back to their folks in China or to provide their children with education which they themselves were deprived of.

Although the USA was the top destination for migrants from China, other countries also received Chinese too. What I briefly described above can equally be applied to the Chinese who decided to immigrate to other countries like Australia and Indonesia, to European countries like the UK and Holland, or to South American countries such as Brazil and Argentina. For a city like Liverpool in the UK, where I now live, it has the distinction of being the site of the oldest Chinatown in Europe, when the Chinese arrived in Liverpool in the late 1850s! They were from Hong Kong and came as seamen employed by one of the most famous shipping lines at the time, called the Blue Funnel. They established a strong trade link between Liverpool, Shanghai and Hong Kong, importing commodities such as silk, cotton and tea. To this day, Liverpool is a twin city linked to Shanghai. The Chinese who came were mainly those living in the New Territories part of Hong Kong.

When I went on a tour to Antarctica in 2016, we had to make a stop at the southernmost city in Argentina called Ushuaia, which has a population of just about 57,000. Out of curiosity, I walked around the small town with my wife, just to get a general feel of this nice, charming and remote place. To my surprise, and with some spontaneous feeling of pride, I saw a fairly new Chinese restaurant in the main street! I did not go in as we were not searching for Chinese food, but I could not help admiring the entrepreneurial spirits displayed by the Chinese, who were clearly immigrants there. That left a permanent image in my memories. So goes the saying: where there are humans, there will be need for food, and where there is a need for food, there will be a Chinese restaurant somewhere close, not only for its exotic flavours, but also for its value-for-money food. For my part, I have nothing but admiration for the earlier Chinese migrants.

More recently, according to information from the International Organization for Migration (IOM, which joined the United Nations to become a Related Organization of the UN in 2016), in 2016 there were about 10 million Chinese migrants living and working overseas and about 1 million international migrants registered in China (a sizable proportion of the latter being returning Chinese from overseas). Chinese form the largest group of documented immigration from a single country in recent history. And, unlike the earlier Chinese migrants in the 19th century, the new generations of Chinese migrants are far better educated, better informed, and with better living conditions. These, plus the well-known Chinese trait of hard work, resourcefulness and tolerance, would ensure they would have a better chance of success than their predecessors.

CHAPTER 8

Emigration from China to colonial Hong Kong post-WW2 – its uniqueness

T he story of migration of Hong Kong is most interesting, probably unique in the migration history of the world. Its uniqueness stands out in many ways.

First and foremost, Hong Kong can never be seen as a destination country, but rather a British colony before 1997. Nevertheless, it was a very popular place for Chinese immigrants due to its geographical location of being situated right at the door of China, and the predominance of Chinese culture in its indigenous population also helped the immigrants from China to assimilate quickly. Currently, nearly all the local population have an ancestral history dating back to generations in China, ever since Hong Kong was ceded to the UK in 1842 as a colony.

Way back in 1842, Hong Kong Island was a small fishing village at the southern border of China with a local population of a few thousand, consisting mainly of Chinese fishermen. Now, by 2022, some 180 years later, the population of Hong Kong is officially registered at about 7.5 million. On this basis alone, one can see and marvel at the scale of its population growth within such a short time.

Yet, the earlier immigration from mainland China to Hong Kong was totally different from other trends of Chinese immigration. For a start, it was primarily a move from one country to a city, which was a colony of a different country. This was unlike all the other Chinese immigrants who moved to other places, as mentioned in the previous chapters, such as the USA, Canada or Europe. Because the population profile in Hong Kong has always been dominated by ethnic Chinese, especially people from Guangdong province in southern China who mainly speak Cantonese (by 2020, more than 95% of the Hong Kong population were of Chinese ethnicity), this means migrants from China over the years have a huge advantage in adapting to life in Hong Kong. Culturally and linguistically, these immigrants to Hong Kong settled very quickly. They do not need to learn to speak another language since the main language of communication in Hong Kong is Cantonese, and in recent years since 1997, the use of Putonghua (Mandarin) has also become prevalent. Even though Hong Kong was a British colony till 1997, such was the way the British governed Hong Kong that the Chinese cultural way of life was respected and preserved. So there is no need to overcome any cultural differences for the migrants from China, the way Chinese migrants to non-Chinese-speaking countries do, as the first hurdle for any migrant is always the language barrier. During the colonial times, all official records of the government were kept in English, but this has not been seen as a deterrent to the progress in Hong Kong. In fact, this actually provided a key incentive for the young people to learn English at school in the colonial education system. I attended the first class in English from my second year in primary school.

By the time Hong Kong reverted to China in 1997, most of the people in Hong Kong could speak English. It is generally regarded that one of the main reasons Hong Kong could achieve its status as one of the international financial centres is the high standard of written and spoken English, especially among the skilled and professional class. These days, most people in Hong Kong are bilingual.

One of the most important factors for any successful migration is the migrants' ability to adapt and assimilate to the culture of the destination country. Here the immigrants from China to Hong Kong post-WW2 had another distinct advantage, which was they did not need to adapt to a different culture in Hong Kong as the traditional culture there was mainly based on traditional Chinese cultures, despite the colonial rule. The emergence of the popular cultures in Hong Kong during the 1980s which made such a mark globally, including martial arts, popular music and film making, were all based on Chinese or Hong Kong culture, mixed perfectly with some western ingredients, but the core was very much Chinese. This was also the main reason why such popular cultures were so widely accepted in China, as the wider Chinese audience felt an easy connection and empathy with the Hong Kong culture. In addition, there are other aspects of traditional cultures which took deep root in Hong Kong, including areas such as the fondness and emphasis of culinary pleasure (Chinese food, even for today, remains the food of choice among the Chinese, both in China and overseas). Festivities such as the Lunar New Year, Mid-Autumn Festival and Winter Solstice have always been the most treasured and celebrated events for the Chinese families. In addition, the idea of the nucleus of a family where members stay together, despite the constraints imposed by limited living space, is still much in place, and it is fairly common to see in Hong Kong that three generations all live together under one roof.

This lesser need for assimilation to local culture was a great enabler for the early migrants in Hong Kong from China. It meant they could start to make a living from the word go, and those who competed with them for jobs and opportunities were also Chinese. It was truly a level playing field for all those who came to Hong Kong. In my view, this was instrumental in the establishment of cultural homogeneity for a young, dynamic and adventurous people, which later helped to develop a competitive advantage for Hong Kong as the society progressed from strength to strength.

Furthermore, the success of the Hong Kong immigrants also helped to attract non-Chinese people from overseas to come to work or invest in Hong Kong. For instance, many British people came to Hong Kong because they saw Hong Kong as a society where it was, until 1997, ruled by the UK, while those from the USA saw Hong Kong as a place where the British rule would ensure the language barrier did not exist, and a legal system that they were comfortable with.

Over a period of time, Hong Kong has been able to change its background as a migrant city to become an international city. In this process, Hong Kong has become a win-win fusion city, arguably the only fusion city in the world where the East and West cultures peacefully co-exist. No other city can boast of such uniqueness.

In the main, there are three factors in the making of this fusion city. First, the migrants from China were able to retain Chinese culture as the core culture. The second is Hong Kong's openness in trade, commerce and tourism, mixed with a sense of eastern exoticism, which makes it one of the most popular tourist destinations in the world. The tourist industry has always been one of the main pillars of Hong Kong's economy. The third is the willingness of people from overseas to come to work in Hong Kong as expatriates, especially in areas requiring special skills. These include corporate executives, lawyers, bankers and accountants. While these expatriates cannot be seen as migrants, they nevertheless contribute to Hong Kong's transformation into a successful fusion city.

Yet it does not mean that Hong Kong, though a very successful story founded on immigration, does not need to have an immigration policy or does not have problems with migration. The Hong Kong SAR (Special Administration Region, officially known since 1997), does have, from time to time, immigration problems, especially the influx of immigrants from China. Population control has always been a source of a policy headache for the government. Over the last 10 years, the population has remained more or less a manageable 7.5 million.

On the other hand, Hong Kong has had its fair share of emigration, with waves of its residents moving away from Hong Kong too.

In 1967, a series of large-scale riots erupted in Hong Kong, causing social instability. These events led some richer Hong Kong residents to move abroad. Emigration took place to countries in Southeast Asia and to Western countries, especially Canada.

The next wave of emigration came when the future of Hong Kong was cast into uncertainty. On December 19, 1984, the People's Republic of China and the United Kingdom signed the Sino-British Joint Declaration and validated that on July 1,1997 there would be the transfer of sovereignty over Hong Kong back to China. The declaration prompted a wave of emigration of the Hong Kong people. This time the popular destination countries were Canada and Australia. In fact, emigration to Canada, especially to Vancouver, in the late 1980s was so popular that a Chinese language TV channel based in Vancouver was at one stage nicknamed Hongcouver!

Many Hong Kong residents were also hoping to settle in the UK. Regrettably, the then British government made it clear – which many judged as immoral – that Hong Kong citizens would not be granted British citizenship on the grounds that residents in a British colony do not carry the same resident rights as a UK citizen. This policy actually was roundly condemned by the people of Hong Kong. It caused a lot of resentments among the Hong Kong people, who saw it as a denial of British moral and political obligations.

In 1989, the Tiananmen Square incident in Beijing triggered a significant emigration wave from Hong Kong through the early 1990s. Canada, Australia, and other Commonwealth countries were the primary destinations for migrants at the time. In particular, popular cities for migrants included Vancouver and the Greater Toronto Area in Canada, Sydney and Melbourne in Australia, and London in the UK. Estimates of the numbers vary widely, ranging from 250,000 to one million people, with the peak years of outflow between 1988 and 1994 of about 55,000 per year. In 1990, the outflow of people reached a peak of 62,000 people (1% of the population). The emigration rate reached the peak in 1992 with 66,000 people, followed by 53,000 in 1993, and 62,000 in 1994.

The main reason cited for the above emigration was the political uncertainty over the historically unprecedented concept of One Country, Two Systems as a model of governance for Hong Kong, agreed and signed by the Chinese and British governments. Many people moved from Hong Kong as they were uncertain about how the situation would play out. But these people were very smart. Often they moved abroad to obtain a residency qualification, but returned to Hong Kong to work. A shining example showing the flexibility and nuances of the Hong Kong people was noted that from 1998, just one year after the transfer of sovereignty of Hong Kong back to China, some Hong Kong-born emigrants with foreign citizenship actually returned to Hong Kong. The phenomenon is called "香港回流潮" (wave of Hong-Kong returnees), so the net loss of population in Hong Kong was reversed. Hong Kong has since enjoyed a stable population of about 7.5 million people.

In 2019, Hong Kong went through another wave of political uncertainty with prolonged local social unrest and protests. So as a result, China had to introduce a new national security law in 2020. The introduction of this law did succeed in restoring order and stability in Hong Kong, but it also led to another wave of emigration from the city. This emigration wave mainly affected those who were thought to be anti-government agitators. One of the most unexpected observations was that, in contrast to the previous wave of emigration from Hong Kong when people had to apply to the destination country for a standard entry visa, this time some countries actually adopted certain specific changes in their legislation to green-light the applications and welcome the people of Hong Kong, with the UK, Canada and Australia being the most accommodating.

A reliable estimate for this latest wave of emigration is very difficult to ascertain as it coincided with the peak of the Covid-19 pandemic when cross-border movements were internationally restricted because of quarantine measures, vaccination requirements and differences in each country's entry and exit requirements.

Another hallmark of the recent trend of migration from China and Hong Kong in the 21st century is that the migrants do not seek to move from poverty. Rather, they move in search of a different life. Those who migrate tend to be the relatively well-off middle class professionals with children. These immigrants are often financially independent, capable of making real and positive contributions to the destination country as an extra source of labour. Just like the last wave of immigration from Hong Kong in 1989, this time the people who immigrate also bring means and skills to the destination country without any fear that they will be a drain on the welfare system. In the case of the UK, there were particular concerns that following the exit of the UK from the EU in 2021, there would be fewer people who could be free to move to the UK to join the labour force, so there would be a skills gap faced by the UK in the next decade or so, especially among the professional classes. The UK, according to the latest figure published in 2021, had a declining total fertility rate of 1.59 children per woman in 2020, down from 1.66 in 2019. It is therefore projected, just like many developed countries, that there is an ageing population and shrinkage of people of working age. Enticing and welcoming professional and young people coming to the UK from Hong Kong is one of the solutions to tackle the possible skills gap. Targeted immigration to import labour is therefore one of the effective tools in any country which demographically may face a dwindling working population.

CHAPTER 9

My own not so interesting story of immigration

I was brought, at the age of three, from Shanghai in China by my parents to Hong Kong. So my parents' story was the start of my family's immigration history. The reason why my father decided to move to Hong Kong was, he told me when I was a child, that he started as a businessman in Shanghai in the 1940s. Then, in 1949, the People's Republic of China was founded. Prior to that, China was torn by civil wars and foreign invasions. The founding of a united China was cheered and welcomed by all. The new government in China was run by the Chinese Communist Party. My father, being a businessman, was concerned that he might be seen as a capitalist and therefore might not be seen as ideologically accepted in this new China. He also had a large family (a wife and six children) to feed and bring up, so he took the decision to immigrate to Hong

Kong, which was then ruled as a colony by Britain, right on the doorstep of southern China.

Life was hard for years, but we did not find it too distressing. We were not alone either, as at the time there were many immigrants from China and most of them found themselves in similar situations as us. Living in relative poverty and insecurity did cause anxiety, but when you saw all those around you were in the same boat, the spirit of camaraderie proved a great help and filled us with some hope. The following ten years were hard but never desperate because in Hong Kong at the time there was a sentiment of optimism with a firm conviction that if we worked hard enough, we would survive and reach our goal. Being poor was always seen as temporary, all of us could break free and make a life for ourselves. So in short, my father's decision to emigrate to Hong Kong was in search of more business opportunities. This gave me my first insight, even as a child, into what immigration means.

Being the youngest in the family, I was therefore lucky assiblings treated me well and looked after me with great affection, something which I shall never forget and always cherish. None of them were able to make it to university due to financial constraints. All of them had to seek work to support the family after high school. By the time I got to the tertiary education age, I was encouraged to apply to Hong Kong University, and luckily I was admitted in 1973 for a five-year course to study medicine.

I then chose to emigrate to the UK in 1980 when I was 26. The reason for this decision was personal, even selfish, perhaps. I wanted to go abroad not in search of a richer life, as the medical graduates in Hong Kong in those days would almost be guaranteed, on graduation, a very high-income job. At the time, Hong Kong was just about to embark on an unprecedented post-WW2 economic boom, which propelled Hong Kong to become one of the internationally famous cities. Life in Hong Kong then was full of promises and opportunities, especially for a professional class such as medicine. By then, all my siblings were working, and they managed to carve out for themselves a reasonably comfortable life through hard work. My brother, who is 18 months older than me, supported and encouraged me to go abroad. He even gave me some start-up money from his meagre savings at the time to help me. He has, of course, completely forgotten about it, and we have never talked about it since. To this day, he is the one person in my world whom I respect most.

The choice for moving to the UK was fairly straightforward for me. I could speak a bit of English, and hopefully my English would get better once I was settled. Hong Kong was a British colony then and my medical degree was recognized by the UK, which meant I did not have to take any test for qualification. The General Medical Council (GMC) in the UK granted me a certificate of registration automatically to allow me to practise medicine.

I was fully aware of the perceived hurdles of immigration, such as racism, inability to settle, lack of cultural adaptability, irrational and unexplainable addiction to Chinese food, and failure to make friends and assimilate into the UK society. I wondered then if I might fail to overcome these hurdles. But I figured also that, since no one forced me to immigrate, and I alone had chosen this path for myself, the onus was on me to try my best to make it work. The last thing I wanted was to arrive in the UK, get a job, but then feel miserable and homesick all the time and fail to settle. In truth, I *was* very homesick, but irrational youthful exuberance saw me through. International telephone calls then were so prohibitively expensive that at the very most I could only afford to call home occasionally and talk for only a few minutes. I resorted to writing diligently and regularly to my mother, brothers and sisters. In those days, the cheapest way was to use a single piece of thin blue paper called an aerogramme, which folded up to become the letter and envelope in one. Nowadays, hardly anyone uses aerogrammes anymore and the young may not even know what an aerogramme is!

On arrival in the UK, my first priority was to start looking for a job. Many doctors in Hong Kong in those days would relish the chance of having a period of four to six years of working in the UK for some postgraduate training and experience in a chosen clinical specialty. This could be done through an arrangement between either the University or the Hong Kong Government and the UK Government, but this overseas training was often limited to one to two years. The chance of being accepted on such a placement in the UK was, needless to say, very competitive and one had to wait for at least five years before one would be considered for such a placement. I did not choose that route. Instead, I decided to try my luck to come over to the UK shortly after I finished my obligatory internship in Hong Kong. On arrival in the UK, I started by sending roughly 150 letters of application. Most did not reply, and the rest wrote to say, with regret, that there was no vacancy.

Then one day, I received a letter asking me to attend an interview for a 2-week locum (a temporary job) in geriatric medicine. On the day of the interview, I was told to report to and wait by the geriatric clinic. After a while, I was called into the clinic, where a male consultant geriatrician was there. He started to ask me some questions, and the tone in which he asked his questions was very patronizing and was even rude, displaying an unmissable air of superiority of lording it over this young, clueless new arrival in the UK for a locum period of two weeks. Clearly, I was the only one being interviewed. By the end of the interview, he asked me brusquely: "So, when can you start? I'd like you to start next Monday" (the interview was the preceding Friday). To that I replied: "No, sir, thank you for the offer, I have decided not to take up the offer." I remember well, to this day, the look of surprise on his face. He clearly had no insight into what my impression of him was during the short interview. I was thought to be so very keen to get a job at his mercy, albeit only a temporary job for two weeks, but I had decided that my integrity and pride could not be compromised.

That was my bottom line. I did not say another word apart from thanking him politely for interviewing me.

One will never know whether the arrogance, rudeness and the air of superiority so apparent in this man was noticed by those who worked with him, though I was sure I was not the only one with that impression. The usual polite word in English to describe such a person was 'pompous'.

On coming out of the clinic, I felt good in the fresh air. That was my first job interview in the UK and, strangely, I felt proud. I could not imagine that I could ever work with somebody like him. But he taught me a useful lesson that in life, whatever one does, one should always have a bottom line. I felt I did the right thing and passed the first test that was thrown at me. I knew I stood to gain from this experience. From then on, I learned that in the art of human interaction, prejudice, pomposity and arrogance should always be avoided at all costs. These qualities are blocks to human progress. On reflection now, many years later, I have a lot to thank him for, as he provided me with the first lesson in how not to behave if one day I became a consultant.

From then on, my career path has been relatively smooth. After three years of postgraduate work in medicine, I was able to enter into a training programme for haematology in the UK and passed two professional examinations. I was appointed as a consultant haematologist in 1989. So it took me nine years to become a consultant. During those nine years, I did not experience any racial prejudice. The UK as a whole was moving towards a more progressive and tolerant society. I got married and have a child. Despite the occasional reports of racial prejudice and social disturbances, the UK as a country is nevertheless moving in a general direction I am comfortable with. The progressiveness and tolerance were not a UK-unique phenomenon – the same can be said of countries in Europe, in the USA, Canada and Australia. These are the key reasons why these countries remain to this day popular countries of choice for immigrants.

My story is just a small footnote to illustrate that the very nature of emigration and immigration can never be as smooth as one would have liked. There will always be roadblocks along the way; more on this in the next chapter.

CHAPTER 10

Expectations of those who emigrate

Naturally, people choose to migrate for different and personal reasons. It is generally accepted that people migrate in pursuit of a better life. But it is often quite hard to define what exactly this better life means in this context. It can mean better employment opportunities leading to better pay and promotion, better social and health services, better chance of personal successes and riches, better personal liberty, and better education prospects for the children. All these reasons are indisputably valid. Often it is a combination of these reasons that compels one to emigrate.

However, I would like to venture a slightly different view, especially in the 21st century, and that is people, more often than not, may decide to migrate for a different life. These modern-day migrants, by and large, may already have enjoyed a certain degree of personal success, acquiring some measure of comfort and security in their own countries. For example, a fair number of British people may have chosen to immigrate to the southern coast of Spain (Costa del Sol) because they would like a sunnier climate near the sea, rather than living in the often cold and rainy weather in the UK. The Irish may choose to move to the UK or the USA. The American Jews may choose to move to Israel. In China, which is now the world's second-biggest economy, there is an emerging middle class with many who may wish to migrate to Canada, the USA, Australia, the UK or Europe. In these days of affordable and convenient international air travel, one common feature of these nouveau migrants is that they are financially secure enough to make visits back to their home countries on a regular basis. Thus they can still maintain a viable link with the folks and friends at home. The previous generations of immigrants did not have this choice, as trips back home could be very expensive or hard to arrange.

In Hong Kong recently, there has been another wave of outward migration of people seeking residency in other countries. This is somewhat unusual and unexpected, since Hong Kong has already metamorphized into a modern metropolis with an international reputation. In the past few decades, Hong Kong was an attractive city for people to move into rather than emigrate from. More people wanted to come in than out, so the government has always had a very tight immigration policy to keep a steady population of about 7.5 million, with immigrants into Hong Kong more or less balanced by emigrants from Hong Kong. However, since the beginning of 2021, there has been a net outflow of people, and up to September, there were 90,000 people who decided to move to the UK alone, a 2.1% drop in the working population. There are others who have moved to Canada, Australia and the USA. Naturally, these figures cannot be properly verified or extrapolated for a projection of the future trend, due to the travel constraints in place for international air traffic to control the Covid-19 pandemic. Nevertheless, this figure cannot be ignored. While it has not led to a significant skill shortage or talk of brain drain in Hong Kong, it is nevertheless a trend that needs to be noted. Already there is talk that in some areas, such as medical services in the public sector, there is an increase in vacant posts due to loss of doctors and nurses to overseas. This shortage has compelled the Hong Kong SAR government to legislate for the granting of practising licences for overseas doctors to work in Hong Kong without taking any licence examinations.

It is generally accepted that this outward migration wave coincided with the introduction of the National Security Law in Hong Kong by China in July 2020. The primary reason for this new law is to bring an end to the significant civil unrest experienced in Hong Kong between June 2019 and June 2020. The introduction of this new law is a source of discomfort and misgivings to some people in Hong Kong who are used to a more open environment where freedom of speech, press and assembly is enshrined. Also, the traditional and standard school curriculum used in Hong Kong has been modified to reflect the changes and progresses made in China since 1949. Some people, especially those with young children, are concerned about such changes in the education curriculum. Invariably, therefore, some people might make a choice to emigrate from Hong Kong. These political developments have also directly led countries such as the UK, Canada, Australia and the USA to relax their immigration policy targeted at the people of Hong Kong. This is like an expression of welcome to those in Hong Kong who may be chewing over the dilemma of staying or leaving. In other words, there is now an easier exit route, a green channel, which was not open to them in the past. This 'welcome with open arms' approach is unprecedented in modern history, since there has always been a very tight immigration policy in these countries. In other words, entry visa to these countries can be granted much quicker with much less bureaucratic and cumbersome checks.

Whatever the rights and wrongs of the political developments in Hong Kong, these countries are undeniably sending a signal of a helping hand to those in Hong Kong who wish to migrate for a different life. Many of these potential immigrants may already be enjoying a middle class lifestyle of some comfort. So, for them, it would involve a significant degree of sacrifice for them to migrate. Many of them, in search of a different life, would have to start all over again in their country of destination. They need to seek the right employment to make a living and to provide for the educational needs of their children. The welcoming hand on offer by these countries is only an entry permit. It certainly does not guarantee success and welfare. Given the reputation of the industriousness and the entrepreneurial flair which the Hong Kong people are famed for in the last 60 years, it is a safe bet to predict that these nouveau immigrants would have a high chance of success and thus make a positive contribution to their new adopted countries. This is also one of the reasons why these countries choose to welcome the immigrants from Hong Kong, who would not be regarded as a burden to their society. Rather, they may bring with them a welcome spirit of dynamism to enrich the local economy.

In Hong Kong, immigration has always been a common topic of conversation for debate and discussion. The concept of immigration is easy enough to understand. If some readers of this book in Hong Kong decide to look around their own families, they will have no difficulties in identifying that, among members of their families, there would be a history of immigration at some stage. The people of Hong Kong have always regarded Hong Kong as a place built by immigrants, mainly from China, especially after WW2, until 1997, when Hong Kong was returned to China. The topic of immigration always guarantees a lively debate over the dinner table. But, it is easier said than done, particularly for those who may contemplate emigrating from a prosperous and modern society like Hong Kong. The idea of emigration can lead to an assumed rosy picture that the grass is always greener on the other side, or it may equally paint a grim picture of descending into being seen as second-class citizens in a foreign environment. The truth is, making a sensible, personal and rational decision on immigration is actually very hard to do. One has to weigh up all the options, not least to answer the question: what if it does not work out?

There are many factors at play. Here, I have personally gone through the full circle. Because of my work in China, the thought did cross my mind if I should migrate back to Hong Kong or China. The deliberations were tough, and, having had the raw and youthful courage to make the first step 40 years ago, I found that I no longer have the same courage to make the reverse journey permanent, despite the obvious attraction that vibrant cities like Hong Kong and Shenzhen have to offer. Age may be the main factor for my lack of courage. I was young, at the age of 26, when I moved to the UK.

The most recent wave of immigration from Hong Kong that started in 2021 is quite different from the last two waves in the early 1980s in the midst of the Sino-British negotiations on the future of Hong Kong. Back then, Canada was uniquely popular, especially for cities such as Toronto and Vancouver. Many experts, mainly solicitors, saw a niche in the market and saw themselves as immigration experts. They set up commercial companies to offer advisory and consultation services for those who wished to leave Hong Kong. By and large, these set-ups served the purpose of providing a general introduction to immigration. They dealt mainly with the processes of applications. Hardly any of these set-ups had the know-how of offering the right advice to their clients. In other words, they did not offer any counselling services even though immigration could set in motion an extraordinary, complex interplay of personal emotions, which would involve professional, domestic, financial, social considerations and, not least, expectations.

These days, managing the expectations of an immigration plan is easier, despite the complex emotions behind such a decision. One of the most effective tools in helping people to manage their expectations in modern days is, though not much reported in the press, the use of social media. We are now all connected in the cyberspace with instant transmission of personal or group messages. Up-to-date information can be freely and readily available, discussed and digested on a ubiquitous mobile device. Such information can actually include videos clips of the living environments, the cost of renting or buying a house, choices of schools, shopping centres and eateries. The average cost of living can thus be easily worked out and budgeted. This undoubtedly is very useful in the minds of any would-be immigrants, so not only can they be as well-prepared as possible, they would also be well-informed of the whereabouts of their contemporaries. A new social group could be formed via group messaging. Information and experiences can be shared and learned. It can also foster a spirit of camaraderie. Furthermore, these new immigrants, instead of congregating to where the traditional Chinatowns are, will actively explore opportunities to assimilate with the local residents in terms of lifestyle and social activities. In fact, the Economist in September 2021 published an article titled The YouTube Immigrants with a subtitle that Britain's new immigrant group (from Hong Kong) is unlike any previous one. This article pointed out how remarkably well-prepared these new immigrants are and how quickly they have adapted to the new home in their new adopted country. In short, the best way to manage one's expectations before making the decision to immigrate is to be well-informed.

I have also been paying close attention to the reaction of the British press to these new immigrants from Hong Kong. In general, the British press and the public reaction are, without exception, quite unanimous in their support for the UK government's policy of granting entry visas to the people of Hong Kong. There have not been any news reports of racial tension or disputes between the native residents and new immigrants. If any, where skirmishes did occasionally flare up, it was usually between the mainland Chinese and Hong Kong Chinese in the UK, who may hold different views of the political problems in Hong Kong.

Another consideration in the thought process is to factor in the question: What if it does not work out, and what is the exit strategy? Unlike the undocumented (illegal) immigrants or those seeking political asylum who often do not have the option of a plan B, the nouveau immigrants do need a plan B. Although most of the new immigrants are probably those with the right skill set and some degree of financial security, plan B is nevertheless necessary. It may require them to have a willingness to restart their career at a lower tier of the career ladder, which means they may need to work their way up, or altogether a different career path such as starting a small-scale commercial enterprise. In my case, I did have a plan B all those years ago. I told myself that if I failed to progress in the UK, I would have to consider moving to Canada or back to Hong Kong. If everything works out smoothly for the immigrants, there is no need to execute Plan B. The need for a Plan B will provide the closure of a complex loop of emotions. It would certainly help to manage expectations. Life, after all, is about options and when it comes to immigration, it is important to have options.

CHAPTER 11

What is the benchmark of success of those who immigrate?

I n my own judgement, the most successful group of immigrants in history is the Jews, though not without blood, sweat and tears experienced by the Jewish people themselves. The reason for this will be discussed later in this chapter. Even prior to the establishment of the nation states, the Jewish people had a long history of migration, from the time of ancient civilizations in Babylon, Judea, Egypt, to a more recent civilization in the European continent. The distinctive feature throughout their thousands of years of history is their mobility as a race. Many of them, just like the Chinese migrants, were persecuted and discriminated, mainly for religious reasons. The dominant religion of most of the places they moved to was Christianity (both the Catholic Church and the Eastern Orthodox), since the Roman Emperor of Constantinople accepted Christianity in 312 AD.

PATRICK CHU

Just before WW2, the Jewish people started to move to the USA and the UK on a massive scale, mainly to escape from the persecution of Jews in Nazi Germany. The migration and immigration of the Jewish people is known as diaspora. This word itself is Greek in origin, meaning 'scatter' or 'spread about'. In fact, the Jewish diaspora was actually mentioned and discussed way back even in biblical times.

The story of the non-Jewish migration is slightly different. It happened as a result of European colonizations, which started roughly from the 15th century. The Europeans from Portugal, Spain, Holland, England, France and Belgium colonized much of Africa, the Middle East, Asia and North America. As a result, the colonized were governed and educated (mainly through the work of Christian missionaries) through a system devised by the colonizers. Their own indigenous culture was then fused with European culture, and invariably, their world view was Eurocentric then. For example, many natives from the Indian subcontinent opted to move to the UK, as India, one of the most populous countries in the world, was then regarded as the Jewel of the Crown for the British Empire. Likewise, many natives of Indonesia, also a very populous country, decided to move to the Netherlands because of its colonization by the Dutch in the 1800s.

Furthermore, Europe was strengthened not only by the two industrial revolutions, but also enriched intellectually and philosophically by the Period of Enlightenment. Many Europeans thus had the knowledge and the skills required

99

in governance, and advancement of economy through trade, commerce and industrial productions. That was the start of the knowledge-based economy. Natives from the colonies, lacking the knowledge of their colonial masters, emigrated to the land of their masters, initially by willingly providing the cheapest form of hard labour that the locals were not willing to do. Then the USA came along in 1776, and since the founding fathers of the USA based their governing principle on the then prevailing European model, both the USA and Europe became popular choices as the countries for migrants. This certainly was the case of the migration of Chinese from the coastal areas in China across the Pacific Ocean to the West Coast of the USA in the 19th century, when China was impoverished and devastated by domestic chaos and foreign invasions.

For nearly all these immigrants, hard labour was what they had to do, but higher aspirations were what they hoped for, for their children. The hope for the success of their children became, therefore, their main benchmark of success.

Each of these waves of migration has their own success story to tell, many of these stories are very moving, reflecting the high ideal of chasing for betterment of life of the human race. One of the most distinguishing features of the success of the Jewish diaspora throughout its history from ancient to modern times is the ability of the Jewish people to keep a high degree of social cohesion among themselves. By that I mean not only can they adapt very well in their chosen country of destination, they can also maintain a high degree of unity within their diaspora community, based on their religious faith (Judaism) and their ties to their ancestral land. In nearly every metropolitan city in the world, there are always synagogues. This is a remarkable tool for the maintenance of their social cohesion, built upon a long history of religious faith.

Chinese diaspora does not have as long a history as the Jewish people, but the number is far greater. It is estimated that in 2019, based on data compiled by the Hebrew University of Jerusalem, there were about 14.7 million core Jews (those who identify themselves as Jewish and do not possess another monotheistic religion), with about 6.2 million of them residing in the state of Israel, while the Jewish diaspora population worldwide was about 8 million, of which 5.7 million lived in the USA. According to figures released by the IOM (International Organization for Migration), the Chinese diaspora, known more commonly as Chinese immigrants, due to its relatively short history compared with the Jewish people, was estimated at a staggering 39.5 million, scattering across 130 countries. These Chinese migrants mainly moved to Southeast Asia, North America and Europe, with the USA having the largest population of them. In the latest figures published in 2016 by Migration Policy Institute in the USA, there were about 2.3 million Chinese immigrants in the country (defined in the USA as foreign-born). For the UK, according to the UK Census 2011, there were just under 400,000 British Chinese in England and Wales (about 0.7% of the population).

Many other immigrants also achieved success and social cohesion in their host countries through faith. The Irish and the Italians made a success of immigration to the USA in its East Coast because of the Catholic faith, even though the USA was founded on Protestantism. More recently, migrants of people with an Islamic faith are also emerging as a successful group.

For the Chinese immigrants, social cohesion is not based on any predominant religious belief, but rather, on shared Chinese culture(s), and primarily on which part of China they came from. Chinese from northern China have a somewhat different lifestyle to those from southern China, and in particular, their dialects are different, though the written language is the same. What actually united the Chinese diaspora was the long cultural heritage and pride in the sophistication of our food and fondness of food – some would even say, our addiction to Chinese food. So, where one can see synagogues for the Jewish people, one sees Chinese restaurants for the Chinese immigrants. This is also the reason why it is common for people to associate Chinatown mainly with its Chinese food. Years ago, when I first moved into my house in Liverpool, I met some of my neighbours and one of them opened her greeting, in a most friendly and unassuming way, by asking which Chinese restaurant I owned! This is a classic case of misplaced stereotyping, a bit like asking a person with a presumed Jewish name such as Jacobs which synagogue he goes to.

So how should one define the success, or failure, of immigration? The answers can be either simple or complicated, depending on who is answering the question. One will get different responses from sociologists, political scientists, historians, economists, politicians or leaders of states.

My answer to that, as a layman who happens to be an immigrant myself, is quite simple. To me, success means three things. First, fulfilment of one's aspirations in a new society which is fundamentally different from home. Second, the ability to be able to assimilate and integrate with the society one is immigrating to, without resentment to the culture of the host country and without forgetting one's own culture. Third, social cohesion, not only between the natives and the immigrants, but among the immigrants too. This is akin to say aiming to get the best of both worlds. There is nothing wrong with this aim, and in fact, I will argue that this is the only aim. This success can lead to a culturally diversified and harmonious society, with enrichment for all. Failure of immigration, therefore, can thus be defined as the inability to assimilate and integrate. Such failure will breed inequality, resentment and social division.

On that basis, one can perhaps draw the conclusion that immigration, as a phenomenon of human endeavour throughout history, is primarily good for human progress. Otherwise, it would not have happened. Immigration opens up the world for all of us, rather than closes us in. Though the internet has successfully helped to link us all up, immigration does predate the internet by a few thousand years. Immigration links us up through the millenniums. However, just like the internet and cyberspace, immigration, if not handled properly, does bring with it some difficulties, especially in recent years. Regrettably, these difficulties, while on the whole do not stem from religions per se, come from the radicalization of certain sects of religious faith through dogmatism and perceived inequalities. As a result, we are seeing the emergence of the dark side with the use of words like crusades, jihadism and infidels. Thus, immigration can often be exploited by political or religious opportunists to serve a very narrow-minded and even nationalistic motive. This will seed social division and help to inflame racism, bigotry, radicalization and even violence, by both sides of the political spectrum. It is paradoxical, even ironical, that while the sharing of a common faith is one of the conditions conducive to the success of immigration, it could also be counterproductive, if abused and exploited politically.

One of the often-quoted benchmarks in assessing the state of a society is the Human Development Index (HDI), first proposed by the Pakistani economist Mr Mahbud ul Haq. He was awarded the Nobel Prize in Economics in 1988. The original model for HDI was a statistical composite index based on life expectancy, education, healthcare and per capita income. These are the parameters we all understand.

Then in 2010, the HDI report introduced an inequality-adjustment known as IHDI. It stated that the HDI should reflect a more modern level of human development. Inequality is thus introduced because it is common in any society, especially inequality for different immigrants of different ethnic or religious backgrounds. So the IHDI has now taken into account the impact of inequality on human development.

Norway, a country which consistently occupies the top spot in both the HDI and IHDI, is a much-admired sovereign country. Regrettably though, even Norway cannot escape its fair share of the problems associated with immigration. In the tragic and notorious incident known as the Norwegian Massacre on 22 July 2011, a lone gunman killed 77 people in a summer camp on one of the Norwegian Islands. Later, he was described as having Islamophobic views and a hatred of Islam. He considered himself as a knight dedicated to stemming the tide of Muslim immigration into Europe. The point to be made here is that in order for immigration to be successful, there is a constant need for tolerance, sensitivity, and political and cultural maturity involving those who immigrate and those who receive the immigrants. Since the millennium, immigration policy has been very much near the top of any agenda in the general elections of every democratic country, as far apart as the USA, the UK, Turkey and Australia. It will be a measure and a test of the statesmanship of those elected to maximize the upside of immigration, while not playing into the fear of the electorate drummed up by those who demonize immigration.

In short, the success of immigration involves fairness, open-mindedness and maturity of three parties, namely the public of the host country, the government of the host country, and the immigrants. If any one of these is found wanting, then immigration is likely to fail and violence would be brewed, with tragic consequences.

CHAPTER 12

How to reconcile immigration with the clash of civilizations

I n 1993, two years after the collapse of the Soviet Union, Professor Samuel Huntington, Director of Harvard's Center for International Affairs at the University, published a paper called "The Clash of Civilizations". The article was a seminal publication, which was widely commented on and debated among the political and academic circles. In 2002, it was expanded and published as a book called "The Clash of Civilizations and the Remaking of World Order". The publication of this book, shortly after the attacks on the World Trade Center in New York on September 11, 2001, was viewed by many as groundbreaking, prescient and relevant. It became a classic text, and it is as influential now as it was then.

On first read, I found the concepts expressed in the book quite hard to comprehend, even hard hitting, and in fact I was only able to read about half the book. A few years later I read it again and began to understand that the thoughts expressed in the book, which predicted that in the future world it would be the cultural, ethnic, religious and ideological differences, and the failure of humanities to reconcile these differences, that would lead to military conflicts and wars. In other words, conflicts and wars would be based on differences in cultures rather than invasion and conquest of territories. Unlike WW1 and WW2, when military expansions and territorial ambitions were the prime reason, wars in the future would be of a different kind, and almost certainly triggered off by different reasons.

The new world order, as he described, would be based on the differences in civilizations on geopolitical, cultural (especially linguistic) and religious grounds. Based on this approach, the world can be separated into different regional civilizations. According to him, it can be viewed broadly as having the following geopolitical components: Western Christian bloc (USA and Europe), Orthodox bloc (Russia), Islamic bloc (Middle East), Latin and South American Catholic bloc, Chinese bloc, Hindu/Buddhism bloc (South Asia), Japanese and African. Each of these blocs manifestly has distinctly different cultures based on languages, race, and religious preferences, therefore each forms the basis for its own core of regional civilizations. For example, the western civilization will be primarily either the English-speaking (USA, Canada, Australia, New Zealand and the UK) or the Christianity-dominated (non-English-speaking Western Europe). The Cold War after WW2 was an entirely different war, as it was primarily an ideological war between the West (representing capitalism) and the Soviet Union (representing communism). Professor Huntington went on to predict that conflicts and wars in the future would be based on clashes of these civilizations and their various ideologies. This clearly has an implication for immigration.

Professor Huntington then published another book, "Who Are We? The Challenges to America's National Identity", in 2004, in which he sharpened his argument that the threat of large scale immigration from Latinos (people from south of the border of the USA, mainly Mexicans) would divide the USA into two peoples, two cultures and two languages (English and Spanish). He proposed that the USA should enact policies that obligate these immigrants to adopt English as their language and Protestantism as their religion to save itself from the threat of Latino and Islamic immigrants. In other words, he initiated a debate on the nature of American identity.

These views were clearly provocative, and were widely criticized by many academics as divisive and rhetorical, calling this work polemic rather than scholarly. Despite this controversy, the views expressed by him should not be easily ignored and dismissed, as they did point out a major issue at the centre of the argument of mass immigration. That issue was: to what extent do the immigrants need to assimilate into the culture of the host country.

The arguments put forward by Professor Huntington would compel countries and policymakers to recognize the importance of carefully managing and controlling immigration in order that any clash of civilizations can be avoided. Furthermore, those who wish to immigrate should also be obligated to respect the culture of the country of destination. This respect can be best manifested by three ways, in the following order. First, awareness of the culture of the host country. Second, acceptance of the culture of the host country. Third, proactive efforts to assimilate into the host country. Adherence to these three criteria does not mean forgetting one's own roots and culture. Far from it, cultural diversities are by no means mutually exclusive. Indeed, in a modern society such diversities not only can co-exist peacefully, but can also add to the cultural enrichment of the society. On the other hand, if these are not handled properly, then it can lead to the host country being swamped with immigrants who fail to adapt and assimilate. The effect would then be bitterness and resentment between both the immigrants and the natives, providing further ammunition for those antagonists of immigration and opportunistic, populist vote-hunting politicians.

Successful immigration and assimilation not only can avoid any clash of civilizations, but can also be an enabler to understand and appreciate various cultures. This will also make significant contributions economically, socially and culturally in the making of a modern society of multiculturalism. The classic successful example of this would be the Jewish immigrants. Without exception, they are able to be successfully assimilated into the culture of the host countries, despite periods of adversity and bigotry. They also make significant contributions in all walks of life to the host countries, and yet, the Jewish people are still able to maintain their cultural heritage, especially the Jewish faith. Equally, other ethnic groups such as the Chinese, Italians, Irish and Indians are also able to assimilate and make their presence felt in the host countries, especially those of the second generation, local-born children of the immigrants.

I have personally felt the benefits of a diversified cultural environment. Ever since I became an immigrant in the UK, which is a very open and tolerant society, I have learned to appreciate the cultures of Jewish people, Indian people and Muslims through learning from and engaging with them both socially and professionally.

If one looks around the world in the 21st century, one can find that in almost all countries, discrimination on the basis of gender, religion, ethnicity and race is not acceptable. It is an indispensable part of human core values in the modern world. For immigration, there may be the occasional skirmishes and tensions between immigrants and natives, but, by and large, these only involve relatively few people and are usually effectively and speedily dealt with. The major tension these days is not related to immigration, but rather tension between races, as the Black Lives Matter movement in the USA in 2020 so clearly demonstrated.

CHAPTER 13

What do we mean by feeling homely ?

A house is not a home, and a home is not a house. A house basically means a building which provides a dwelling for the occupants, while a home is much more personal for the occupants. Implicit in the word homeliness, there is a feeling of belonging to, or having the characteristics of a home, which can provide a relaxed and personal environment with familiarity, intimacy, comfort, freedom and safety, thus leading to a feeling of homeliness. The attainment of this feeling of homeliness can be used as a benchmark for successful immigration. This explains why in most countries, the ministry that deals with their people is called the Home Office, and matters of immigration fall under the remit of the Home Office.

This sense of homeliness, it must be stressed, cannot be achieved overnight, and cannot be bought by money, by power or by influence, which can only assure comfort, and even luxury, but not the relaxed state of freedom and intimacy that homeliness can bring. The attainment of homeliness is an insidious process, and to achieve this takes time and effort. In the process of attaining this sense of homeliness, there will be hardships and challenges along the way, such as matters of employment, education and financial security. These can only be handled with perseverance, flexibility and the ability to adapt. Nothing worthwhile in life can be achieved overnight, otherwise it is just luck. To reach the state of homeliness, the toughest part is usually at the beginning, as it often means a personal journey from nothing to something.

Here I would like to share a bit more with the readers about my own story. When I first came to the UK, I had no idea of how restricted the opening hours of the shops were, no idea where to get groceries and from which shops. The public transport system was minimal (as most people had cars). So, I had to start with the very basics, and ate nearly every meal in the hospital where I worked. In the beginning, I was only interested in the news from Hong Kong, which could be very difficult as the only way to get such news in those days was to buy the very expensive edited version of Hong Kong newspapers in Chinatown. Slowly but surely, I started to assimilate into my new environment. And it was my good fortune that, being a doctor, I got to interact with many people from various backgrounds, all working in a hospital environment. Gradually, without me making much conscious effort, I began to pay attention to the news in the UK. I began to adapt to the minutiae of British cultures such as pubs, fish and chips, steak and kidney pies, and beans on toast. Above all, greeting everyone by commenting on the weather first, such as 'What a lovely day' or 'What a miserable day'! This was always a social icebreaker.

Perhaps I have been lucky in my relatively smooth immigration journey. I was then single and within three months I was able to get a temporary job as a doctor, after which I was offered a permanent job. My career has been relatively smooth too. I started to learn more about the UK way of socializing by going with colleagues to the pubs after work, otherwise known as the Happy Hour, and I got to experience traditional Sunday roast lunch through invitations from British friends (I thought it was funny how such traditional Sunday lunch usually starts at around 3pm!) and I got used to having sandwiches for lunch. I also found out, most amazingly, that the British do not call the British currency 'pound' (they used the word only in writing) but call it 'quid'! When I first heard of the word, I had to ask my colleague what the word quid meant. When I worked in Northern England, I learned that people call the meal you eat at lunch time 'dinner' and the meal you eat at around 6 pm 'tea'! So imagine my confusion when a colleague asked me around lunch time to go for dinner! Gradually, I began to love the traditional British dish of fish and chips, where the fish is deep fried in crispy batter and the chips are chunky, soft inside and crispy outside, unlike the French fries which are thin. I even started to add salt and vinegar to my chips, which is a unique way of the British eating their chips. The famous British fried-up breakfast, consisting of fried eggs, fried tomatoes, fried bacon, fried sausages and fried toast, quickly became another one of my weaknesses, though I gave them up after a few years as they are so manifestly bad for the health. When I have visitors from China and Hong Kong, I would make a point of taking them out for fish and chips, in addition to the obligatory Chinese meals. I maintain this habit to this day.

Then a few years later, I bought my first house and my first car (which was an eight-year-old fourth-hand Volkswagen; the model was so old that they stopped making it about 15 years ago). My house was small and every piece of furniture in it was a sort of self-assembled cheap DIY (do-it-yourself) stuff, and the kitchen cooker was also second-hand. The only new gadget I had at the time was a washing machine, as I had no time to do the washing. I could not afford a television either, so instead I rented one of the cheapest models with a 14-inch screen, which was round and bulky in those days. On weekends, I would go to the local Chinese supermarkets to get some groceries to experiment with cooking Chinese dishes. In those days, long distance phone calls were something only the rich could afford, so instead I wrote many letters home to my mother and siblings. This was the time when I started to feel both at home and homely. The house became my home. As the feeling of homeliness in that little tiny dwelling of mine started to creep into the state of my mind, it helped me hugely in coping with my homesickness. I was even able to invite my mother to visit and stay on several occasions over the years.

For me, it was a hard time material-wise, but it was a precious and memorable time. There was the feeling of being free and independent in my own small world. A feeling of homeliness came over me every time I came back to my small and sparsely decorated home after a hard day's work. That was when I knew the difference between feeling homely and homesick – the latter is mainly about your families back home. Now, the UK is my home. I have never regretted once that I have immigrated to the UK, especially in fulfilling my aspiration to be trained as a haematologist.

So, without making much of a self-conscious effort, I was able to assimilate myself into the British way of life. I have British friends of various ethnic backgrounds and have greatly enjoyed their friendship. I cherish the cultural diversity this can offer, from India to the Middle East to Africa, while also getting to know people from Ireland to Scotland and Wales. It feels like a big family.

Professionally, I have experienced no difficulties or barriers in looking after my patients or dealing with their anxious families. It is also gratifying for me that my patients and colleagues seem to accept me as well. I can hardly remember any racial slur on me, though even if there had been any, I would almost certainly have ignored it, better still would have forgotten it, for the simple reason that this was so crass that it is better to forgive and best to forget.

Life affects different people in different ways. While many immigrants would share similar stories to mine, many others would have a much harder story to tell. They may have come with young children, with the additional stress of finding a suitable placement for their children in school. They may have difficulties in establishing a firm career path. For various reasons, it may take them longer to assimilate into society. In my own professional circle, I have met many immigrants and indeed in my professional capacity, I have appointed many of them into the National Health Service in the UK. These were mainly doctors and nurses from the Middle East and India. I still keep in touch with many of them since I left the NHS, and without exception, they seem to have settled down well, too, in this their country of destination.

Ten years ago, I was invited to go to help out in a new hospital in Shenzhen, a mainland Chinese city near the border to Hong Kong. It was like a replay journey, but in the reverse order. I had to assimilate again, though this time it was far easier as I am an ethnic Chinese and have not forgotten some basic Chinese ways of life. The only difference is that, this time, I do not have a house or flat (too expensive) or a car (not necessary)!

CHAPTER 14

What are the outlooks for immigration and the potential migrants?

L ike it or not, immigration has always been regarded as an issue which, to the bigoted, has a racist tone. Unfortunately, this is almost unavoidable, as it always tends to involve people of a certain race moving to a destination land dominated by people of a different race. So, it is often difficult for any country which is popular as a destination for immigration to have a fair and humanitarian immigration policy due to domestic resistance from those who oppose inward migration of people from a different race. In addition, many of those who seek to move tend to be the lower and middle income group moving to the richer countries with a more advanced economy and a higher per capita income, such as the USA, Canada, the UK, member states of the EU,

Canada and Australia. Some rich oil states in the Middle East, such as Saudi Arabia and United Arab Emirates (UAE), are also popular. According to the United Nations, Saudi Arabia was the third most popular country, and UAE the sixth, for immigration in the world in 2021. The latter two countries are unique. Unlike other major economies, Saudi Arabia and UAE are not only cash-rich from their oil producing abilities, but they also have very ambitious infrastructure projects aimed at modernizing their countries. As such, they need to attract immigrants to provide the much-needed infrastructure labour force. Many of the Western countries also have similar problems with labour shortages, which could be hard to solve as these countries also have demographic concerns of reduced fertility rates and an ageing population, implying their labour shortage would be an ongoing issue.

One country which needs special mention when one is discussing the outlook for immigration is Japan. Japan has a population of 125.8 million and has the world's third-largest GDP in 2022. In fact, Japan's economy was the world's second largest (behind the USA) from 1968 to 2010, when it was overtaken by China. Unlike other advanced economies, Japan has always been a country which was not open to immigration. It has an ageing population which shows no sign of easing. In 1965, the proportion of those above 60 years of age was less than 10% of the overall population and in 2015, the proportion has increased to about 40%, and by 2065, it is estimated that around 60% of the population will be more than 60 years of age. Meanwhile, its fertility rate dropped from 2.1 in the 1970s to around 1.4 currently. Japan also has one of the world's longest life expectancies of around 85.5 years. Given this demographic time bomb, the Japanese government changed its hitherto very restricted immigration policy to an active one in 2018, with an immigration target of 300,000 over five years. Even with that initial target, it still had to quickly adjust the figure upward in 2019 to 345,000 over the next five years, particularly in sectors like farming, construction and nursing. This immigration target will account for about 0.5% of the country's working population of 67 million.

Faced with the multitude of factors such as race, financial need of the immigrants, labour shortage and reduced fertility, most of the economically advanced countries therefore would generally have their own managed immigration policy, which by and large is acceptable to the natives. The policy in these different countries has one thing in common. It is primarily based on a quota system to cap the total number of immigrants allowed in each year and a scoring system to assess if the skills offered by them match the needs of the country. So, in short, both the number and the skill set of the immigrants allowed are controlled, to the advantage of the host countries. The only exception is the EU, where the people in the current 27 member states can move freely, without any restrictions, within the EU boundary. The movement of the people within its member states is not regarded as immigration, but rather free migration. While this freedom of movement within the EU has come under attack by some political and media sectors within the EU, no other regions (consisting of many states) in the world offer such freedom to their inhabitants. For me, this is the greatest strength of the EU – which used to have 28 member states, but the UK opted to leave the EU officially in 2021 with the freedom of movement within the EU being one of the main reasons cited by the UK for leaving.

In recent years, an unusual situation has occurred pertaining to the situation in Hong Kong. Hong Kong was a British colony until 1997, when it was handed back to China and has since been governed under the One Country, Two Systems Principle enshrined in the Basic Law jointly agreed by China and the UK. The essence of this agreement is to provide a significant degree of autonomy for Hong Kong in running its own affairs for up to 50 years. However, following some turbulent civil unrest and disorders in 2019, in which some people took to the streets to demand political changes to allow for more democracy, a New National Security Law was introduced in Hong Kong by China in July 2020. This new law has led to a great number of people who advocated freedom of speech and democracy being arrested, detained and imprisoned in Hong Kong. They are seen as political activists under foreign influence working against the interests of China. Confidence in the judiciary is seen by many in Hong Kong as being compromised. In addition, the education syllabus has also been changed to reflect the desire of the government that more should be taught about modern China than the previous curriculum. Hong Kong, prior to this law, enjoyed freedom of speech and press, and an independent judiciary with many of the appointed high court judges from London. So the implementation of the new National Security Law and the changes in the education and judiciary systems proved to be very unsettling in the eyes of some people, especially those with young children. They face a very different future and thus may wish to emigrate. No one knows how the events will turn out in the next few years in Hong Kong, especially with the travel restrictions and hazards brought by the Covid pandemic. Predictions are made by commentators and economists that there may be further emigration from Hong Kong after the pandemic is over and travel restrictions removed.

Because the events in Hong Kong have made international headlines since 2019, countries (the UK, Canada, Australia and the USA) I mentioned in the previous section have modified their immigration policy by extending a welcoming hand to people from Hong Kong. They offer those who wish to immigrate a unique fast-track green channel. In short, immigration has now become much easier for the people of Hong Kong, unlike the previous waves of immigration from the city.

Early indications published in the Times of London with data obtained from the British Home Office showed that for the first nine months of 2021, there was a net outflow of Hong Kong emigrants and 90,000 applications were approved during this period, though the trend cannot be fully ascertained until the Covid pandemic is over. My own guess is that Hong Kong is likely to have another wave of emigration once the Covid-19 pandemic has receded.

For the people from other countries who wish to emigrate, the gatekeeping mechanism for obtaining entry visas to the above-mentioned countries remains the same. Gaining entry to these countries is possible, but is still very difficult. There is no such equivalent fast-track system, as far as I am aware, offered by these countries except for the people of Hong Kong, due to the unique political changes since the social unrest in 2019.

Altruistic reasons apart, the people from Hong Kong are also thought of in the West as smart, hardworking, self-independent, resourceful, adaptable and, above all, very law abiding. As such, they are far more likely to settle down in the host countries and become productive members of society. They are unlikely to be a drain on the welfare systems of the host countries. They and their children can make meaningful contribution to the host countries. After all, this is what immigration is all about, that both sides can benefit.

CHAPTER 15

The age of hyper-connectivity's impact on immigration

T his chapter will explore what effects the modern age of cyber hyper-connectivity has on immigration, in particular by asking the questions: does it make immigration easier, and if so, in what way?

On the whole, I think hyper-connectivity does make immigration easier. As far as the process of application, verification, data collection, background checks are concerned, they can be done and stored with great ease and involve much less human effort. For a would-be immigrant, this can be seen as the same process as an electronic application for a travel visa or a mortgage in buying a house. This is now much more convenient, efficient and faster. Data automation and artificial intelligence with well-designed algorithms will see to that. The process is also trackable, auditable in real time. It can provide instant updates and cross-references. The information can also be more securely stored by cloud technology.

This does not, however, mean that the approval of an immigration visa is easier. Far from it: the electronic process can render the process more elaborate and thorough, especially where the provision of personal financial details and professional background is concerned. For instance, these days, if I wish to apply for immigration and state that I am a medical practitioner, I would have to state my professional qualification and practising licence with the General Medical Council in the UK, which can be easily cross-checked by the processing authority of the country to which I would like to immigrate. In early 2021, when the British government granted the fast track green light to Hong Kong residents who were born locally before 1997 and hold the British National Overseas (BNO) passport, it was explicitly stated by the British Home Office that the applicants could apply online rather than going to the British Consulate in Hong Kong. So, there is an extra level by which the privacy of the applicants can be protected and any visits to the consulate and interviews can therefore be kept to a minimum. In early 2022, the UK government announced that those born in Hong Kong after 1997 are also eligible to apply.

Prior to the age of the internet, there were, in Hong Kong at least, commercial set-ups which provided special immigration advice. These set-ups were familiar with the immigration rules of most popular countries such as the USA, Canada, Australia, the UK and Europe. They were popular in Hong

Kong, blossoming particularly during the last major waves of emigration back in the early 1980s. They had specific information for each country, thus they were able to provide all-round advice based on the special situation of any given applicant, and often they were able to provide the necessary legal advice too.

Then all started to change, at lightning speed, because of the internet and digitalization. We are all benefiting from the age of instant information and 24-hour services, such as international banking and booking of airline tickets (a service which was almost monopolized previously by travel agents). As a result, such immigration advice centres have all passed their sell-by date. There is now no need for such special set-ups, and they don't work 24/7 anyway! The new generation of would-be immigrants are now very well-informed because most of them are very accomplished netizens. As such, they can be very well-prepared. All the necessary governmental information on immigration policy in any country is now online, with clear and authoritative instructions. Not only that, other supplementary and important information, such as education, accommodation, medical services and employment opportunities, is all freely available in much the same way. So, in theory, therefore, any would-be immigrants can still work full-time during the week, needing only a few evenings at the keyboard, and the information obtained may be more comprehensive than any immigration advice centre could have offered. So modern technology can enable them to manage their expectations even before they set foot in the host country.

Another real advantage that cyberspace can offer is instant P2P messaging, or even group chat forums like WhatsApp. Every one of us these days may know someone who is already an immigrant, or someone who may wish to be one. Such P2P messaging helps to provide the necessary intelligence and information, based on personal experiences, in addition to the generic information online. This can help to relieve the anxiety and clear up the uncertainty faced by the applicants. All immigrants are by nature first timers; there are no seasoned immigrants. The better prepared the immigrants are, the quicker it would be for them to get settled in their new environment.

For me, when I moved to the UK, I did not have any advice or network to help or advise me. But now, I myself have been asked on many occasions by friends on personal social forums about the situation in the UK. I always try my best to provide them with what I think is relevant and impartial advice. Such advice can vary from the cost of a two-bedroom flat in a specific residential area, the average weekly cost of groceries, the standards of the local schools, to job opportunities, such as for doctors in any chosen area for the applicants. I have also been asked on several occasions about the property prices near where I live and even the cost and the process involved in building home extensions, the availability of painters, builders and decorators! This information superhighway will help to make their new life as immigrants much more predictable. It is quite easy for them to work out a basic weekly grocery bill, for example, by visiting the various supermarkets online.

In short, a well-prepared individual or family can reasonably expect to come to a country like the UK and soon after arrival can start looking for more suitable accommodation, become well acquainted with the local amenities, enrol their children for schools, register with their general practitioners, find a job, then perhaps even seek permanent accommodation in an area of their choice. The internet enables them to start this preparatory process even before they buy their airline tickets! I know a few families who achieved all these aims within six months of their arrival. It is particularly encouraging also, on my regular phone chats with them, that they all seem to have settled down very quickly, far quicker than I did all those years ago. For their social life, many of them already have some friends who have also immigrated, so they form a social group to enjoy the camaraderie with their contemporaries. They know their neighbours, know the local Chinese supermarkets (a must for Chinese all over the world!), and most importantly, their children are very happily and quickly settling down in their new schools. They tell me that their children are very happy for two reasons. One reason is that they have much less homework! The other reason is that not only do they make new friends, they also have 'old' friends who arrived in the UK almost at the same time, living close by. These new immigrants give me the impression that they are adjusting to their new life well. I hope they can soon find their home homely.

Modern day hyper-connectivity offers another distinct advantage by enabling the immigrants to maintain a very close link with their families and friends back home, with instant real time video chats either as an individual or a group, as videoconferencing and group chats are now the new normal since the Covid-19 pandemic. Instant communication between the immigrants and their families back home is available 24/7, and the only thing they need to consider here is the time difference. Nothing else stands in their way. It is cheap and thus easily affordable too. This would be the new normal for them. I have also personally found this modern hyper-connectivity most useful and rewarding, since for the last six years, even before Covid-19, I have been videoing almost daily on two time zones (life in the UK and work in China). I found that I can manage to continue to work for my hospital without too much difficulty.

CONCLUSION

I n the history of humanity, migration of our ancestors was always a fact of life for them. Our ancestors always had to move to a better habitat with more favourable climate and better availability of food. It was a natural and basic instinct, in accordance with Darwin's Theory of Evolution. During this evolutionary process, our ancestors occupied the top of the food chain by becoming complex social beings. This ability to interact with our fellow beings helped us to develop a high level of social intelligence. This evolution progression began much earlier, before the emergence of ancient civilizations, which heralded the beginning of the establishment of an ordered and structured society. The migration and the herd instinct (our preference to be with other human beings) of our ancestors conditioned humans to realize that survival and progress depended on the coexistence with each other. Thus, humans have learned that the need to cohabitate was imperative right from the dawn of civilization.

Ancient civilization began some 5,000 years ago along the Rivers Tigris and Euphrates (present day Iraq). There were, roughly, at around the same time, many other civilized regions as well, from China to India to the American continents. The common hallmark of all these civilizations was one of migration, adaptation and assimilation. Humans do kill each other through tribal fightings or even large scale wars, but these were and still are, sporadic in nature. What is perpetual is our need to live with one another.

Immigration, however, is a more recent development in name only. It occurs only after the establishment of nationhood, where we have countries, with each defined by its territory and sovereignty. As more countries are formed and some became prosperous, what was known as migration in the past is now known as immigration.

While migration is natural and uncontrolled, and occurred mainly in the past as a necessary phenomenon for human development, immigration, however, is a controlled phenomenon. In the past, migration did not have restrictions except those imposed by the barriers of nature in providing a suitable habitat for humans, such as high mountains, lack of farmland, extreme temperatures or shortage of water for irrigation. The restrictions on immigration, however, are man-made. It depends on permission by the natives. In modern times, migration and immigration are more or less viewed by some as an interchangeable concept. The one distinguishable feature is that migration nowadays can only occur freely and unchallenged within a sovereign state, while immigration means entry visas to a different sovereign country defined by territories. In that sense, migration is a freer and reversible process, while immigration is much harder since it requires the permission to enter another country and is often just as hard to reverse.

Because immigration is a harder process, so it is more imperative that the desires, the motives and the determination of those who wish to immigrate need to be understood clearly by both the immigrants and the host countries. No one in life would choose to do things the hard way unless there are compelling reasons to do so. These reasons can be social, personal and financial. The strength of these feelings can help them to deal with the hardship and challenges along the way. In other words, immigration is not for the faint hearted. So, when it comes to moving to a different country, migration and immigration can be regarded as the same thing. Immigration represents the beginning of the process, while migration represents the process itself, before successes and failures can be judged.

On this basis, I would suggest that immigration should in general be viewed as a natural social phenomenon, with all the tension, anxiety, problems and joy that any social phenomenon would entail. In the long run, immigration, if successfully managed, can be beneficial to both the immigrants and the host country. No resources can be as precious and versatile as human resources. On that basis, one can draw the conclusion that no countries in the world actually reject immigration, but rather, each has its immigration policy based on its own consideration of the balance of demands for extra human resources and the tolerance of its indigenous population. None is more so aptly demonstrated than the USA, which was founded after the 13 colonial states on its east coast sought independence in 1776. Within 100 years, its territory stretched from the Atlantic Ocean to the Pacific Ocean. It has also become, for many, the de facto New World and by far consistently the most popular country in the world as the country of destination for immigrants.

No man is an island. The story of Robinson Crusoe is a fiction, however popular that story may be. Such an isolated way of life described in that wonderfully entertaining book is not the norm and will never be the norm. It is the romantic expression of a lifestyle that most of us, if not all of us, would not choose to live, even though some of us may just fantasize about it. We are all part of the society we live in. Hermits are the exception, applicable only to a few, while the rest of us are gregarious.

The views expressed in this book may not be adequate, both in its breadth and depth. There will be unknowing and therefore, unintentional, omissions or inadequate discussions on facts and figures. Such detailed discussion can best be left to the learned scholars, political scientists and historians. Nevertheless, it cannot be disputed that immigration is always a very sensitive and emotional subject. There are protagonists and antagonists, each with their perfectly valid views. These views and discussions can be heated and biased, but they cannot be distracted from the key fact that immigration is here to stay. It can be managed and controlled, but it cannot be extinguished.

To the best of my ability, writing as I do from the point of an immigrant myself, I try to be honest, impartial and without any prejudice. For me personally, I feel fortunate and blessed that I could become an immigrant and have adapted reasonably well to my country of destination. Others less fortunate than me may have a different story. By and large, I believe that their successes are far more common than their failures.

Our very presence in the world requires us to be social beings, to accept others rather than reject them. The greatest catastrophes of human conflicts in history are the two world wars, with an estimated total death toll of about 80 million, including those who were counted as missing. Both wars arose from military conflicts between alliances of different countries based on their needs, or greed, in the acquisition of power over others and territorial expansion. No historians have ever put forward that immigration, migration, racial or religious bias was part of the causes of these two world wars. Nazi Germany committed crimes against humanity in the holocaust, but Nazi Germany did not invade others because of the Jewish people; it invaded others because of its desire to achieve power, control and territorial expansion at the expense of other sovereign nations.

Our existence in this world means that we must learn to live with one another. We may be liked or disliked as individuals, but collectively one must have the ability to tolerate and accommodate our fellow human beings, wherever they are from. This is not speaking from riding on a moral high horse. Far from it, it is just basic common sense that to live in this fast-changing world, the Darwinian principle is such that for us to improve, we need to adapt.

Humanism is a philosophical stance that emphasizes the potential and agency of human beings, individually and socially. It considers human beings as the starting point for serious moral and philosophical inquiry. Immigration, however uncomfortable it may be for some, is such an issue for humanism. As I am putting my finishing touches to this manuscript, I cannot help but notice that the world has been in the grip of wave after wave of infection by Covid-19 and its variants. No country has managed to escape the virus. It is the first pandemic we have experienced in living memory. Each country is fighting its own battle to contain the outbreak. No country is gloating about its success, nor hiding its shortcomings and fears. One thing is clear: each country wishes to learn from the others by sharing the information and data on how to vaccinate, when to vaccinate, and what else can one do to stay away from infection. For this reason, some view that Covid-19 is a great leveller, it levels all of us into thinking in a similar mindset and thus taking similar actions and precautions. I do agree with this view. Suddenly, immigration has become a silent subject as fighting the pandemic is rightly top of the agenda. But immigration will not be a silent subject for long. No doubt the debate on the rights and wrongs of immigration will resurface again, but at least one can hope that the discussion then will be on a much more mature and rational level. That is the aim of this book.

"Maybe it is the instinct of every immigrant, born of necessity or of longing: Someplace else will be better than here. And the condition: if only I can get to that place!"

Christina Henriquez, The Book of Unknown Americans